Practicing Mindful Living

Dr. Debra Webb

Enjoy retirement — this is the
perfect time to practice mindful
living!
      Best Wishes!
         Debra

First published by Dog Ear Publishing
4011 Vincennes Rd
Indianapolis, IN 46268
www.dogearpublishing.net

ISBN: 978-1-4575-4673-0

This book is printed on acid-free paper.

Printed in the United States of America

My husband's continual support and encouragement helped me believe in putting my voice out into the world, and his example helps me practice mindful living every day.

This book is dedicated to my daughters and grandchildren, in hopes that they practice mindfulness in their daily lives. Ryan and Erin, you are loved.

Introduction

Mindful living is the practice of becoming aware of your surroundings and aware of your thoughts and feelings each day. The purpose of practicing mindful living is to opening yourself to your potential for creating a better place for yourself, your family, your community and our world. Each day we are given the opportunities to practice this awareness.

The sections of this book are set up to correspond to the twelve months of the year, with each month focusing on an important aspect of living fully with joy. Each month provides ideas for engaging in living a full life, as well as activities for making changes in your personal life.

January leads you to examine the many cycles and patterns within your life and how to leverage those cycles. The month of February will have you work toward balancing your mind, body, and spirit. March focuses on family relationships, and April will engage you with working on choice. Nurturing yourself and others is the work of May. The month of June focuses on celebrating aging. July guides you to study being a leader in your family, workplace, and community. August offers a chance to work on the skills of practicing forgiveness. September prompts you to think about the courage needed to live your destiny. Compassion is explored as an important living skill in October. November engages you in acting on gratitude, and December helps you work through endings and being open to new beginnings.

Practicing Mindful Living examines many areas of living and is flexible to allow you to follow your own journey of opening your mind, body, and spirit to possibility.

You do not have to start with January or follow a month-by-month sequence. Let your learning and reflective needs guide you to move through this book as you need.

January

January meets the end of the year and starts a new beginning. It is a month to think about all the varied cycles and patterns that we engage in during our daily routines and habits.

Examining all cycles, from family ties to how we eat dinner, can provide us insight, opportunity for change, and time to honor what works. We spend our lives spinning through the same thinking, habits, and people, so take January to examine what works and what does not work in your current patterns.

During the month of January, when old meets up with new, it is time to rejoice in those cycles that bring you happiness and health while making meaningful adjustments in those cycles that leave you unproductive.

January Focuses

Identify important cycles and patterns.

Be open to the change process.

Make meaningful and purposeful adjustments.

January 1

The cycle of life
   Pushes and pulls
Each through every life interval
   Pacing develops our inside face
Shaking, Shaping, Swallowing
   We emerge, become present
And wrinkle
Solitary, joined, and then alone
   No path the same and yet each
Similar
Never understood fully
   Stripped, Shared, Severed
We begin and end.

The month of January begins a new cycle in the form of a year, but cycles are a significant part of our every day lives. You will find them in people and nature. Taking time to understand your cycles and patterns will help you understand your place in the larger world.

While your own cycle shapes who you are, being aware of your habits of thinking and living allows you to make adjustments to your patterns. Leveraging the positive and breaking the negative are important to growing throughout your life.

Today, begin to list your patterns for examination—think both big and small. As you list your patterns, identify what is healthy and happy, and which one or two areas need adjusting.

January 2

Nature circles around us

At times gentle caresses and at times

Harsh slaps

A long life begins to see

Part of the circle

A beginning and an end

Just as nature leaves a mark in the

Rings of trees or

In the canyon stone

We make our own mark

Our footprint

It matters

To the circle

Changing, conducting, converging

Marking those continuing.

As you move into a new year, take a look at the marks nature has left on your heart, soul, and body. Do not consider the caresses and slaps that nature provides as anything but part of your own circle of life. Cherish them all.

Each year is another circle that imprints who we are. It stamps our footprint on this earth, and each footprint matters in the journey of life.

Take stock of those new marks—a new love, a new set of wrinkles, or a new perspective. Embrace each with love and care as you start a new circle.

January 3

Life cycles through you, pulsing
    And pushing
Each inhale to reach the
    Next breath
It mirrors your own daily cycle of
    rising and falling.
What in the cycle matters?
    The circle of life's blood racing
Through
    For the next cycle to resurface,
Or the cut that breaks the cycle
    And demands a shift?
Which takes more living—
    The undisturbed cycle or the
cut?

Take this time to contemplate your daily routines and habits. Examine them and determine which need to be continued and which need to be broken for you to be healthy and whole. Living a full life includes painful times, but *deciding* to live fully and *owning* your living is freeing.

There are positive aspects of undisturbed routines. Those routines provide continuity and comfort. They also can put us in a stagnant state of no growth. Simple shifts in our routines can spurt creativity and a new mindfulness about life. Cutting a habit or routine of comfort, whether it is in tradition, relationship, or something as simple as a change in the route you take to work, is difficult. Cutting allows us to use our resiliency and to determine new paths for the next cycle of thinking.

Be courageous and determine which undisturbed routines give you strength and which need to be cut. Develop a plan to maximize your new beginning.

January 4

There is a rhythm in the calendar
My focus for thirty years.
The weeks and months
Defined
My movement and thinking.
The calendar is a comfort
My body and mind respond
In time with it.
I sense the calendar closing
Its final year, month, and day.
I am unsure.

Whatever your work, most likely, there is a cadence or routine that your mind and body respond to every day. There is a comfort in this routine for many. For a teacher, when a bell rings, it is time to move. There are similar routines in every profession. Adjusting to a new routine offers excitement and fear.

As time for new routines comes, it is normal to be fearful. To work through the fear, you need to let your body and mind examine the new routine, breathing with the new timing of life.

Take this moment to examine your routines. Know that there will come a time for it to change; be ready to breathe with the change. Be thoughtful about your plan for the transition.

January 5

Waves rush forward
And then move back
Bringing new treasures
For those sifting
Through the sand
Like time rushes
Around me
I leave treasures
For those to pick through
And then wait for the rush
To sweep me to the sea.

It is important to meaningfully think about what you are leaving, not at the end of your life but in each part of your day.

Life comes to us in twenty-four-hour segments, and we are responsible for the treasures we leave for others. At the end of today, review what you are leaving for others. The best part of life is that a new cycle starts each day and, we have the opportunity to make someone smile or to give to someone without expectation or acknowledgment.

Be intentional in your twenty-four-hour cycle to leave something positive. Over the next week, track what you are leaving to others. Be determined to improve the quality of your gifts.

January 6

Opening to

My personal

Adaptation

Of looking

At the steps

I take in

Life

Moving out

Stagnant, stale

Paths crossed

Willing

To take an unknown

Step on my path.

The start of a new year brings each of us the possibility to be open to change. Start by reviewing your current habits to develop a change plan. Being able to adapt is what gives us hope.

To stay young, we should continually refresh by reframing our thoughts and actions. For us to adapt to a new way of thinking or a new habit, it must be identified, the old habit undone, and the new habit created. It is important to be intentional with the changes we change.

Don't try to change everything, but focus on changing the one or two habits that might provide you happiness and hope. When you undo the old habit, be mindful and stay your course. Your method of creating a new mindset should be thought out.

January 7

Life is a renewal process
Each day allows us to regenerate
A new week frees
Us from previous faults
A new month is filled
With possibility
To change course,
Opening opportunities
To tackle,
Renew with joy
Each moment.

Believing in renewal is the first critical step to continued growth as a person. A year can seem so long, with so much time to put off what can be done day by day.

On this day, free yourself from those things that have kept you from fulfilling your regeneration. Don't get stuck in the past but look forward to the possibilities of today.

Intentionally, with mindfulness, start today with the intention to tackle new opportunities—weight loss, a bad habit, or negative thinking—not with dread of past failures, but with joy that today is a new opportunity to make the shift. Cycle through this year with daily renewal—being mindful should never get old.

January 8

My world shifts

While I am

Unaware

So I vow

To be aware

Of my world

In order to give

Gratitude for

Events and people

Leaving

Paths

Unknown to me.

I will say good-bye

And smile

For I am fortunate

To have had the

Experience.

Transitioning is difficult and requires a process or an ending ceremony. When we complete transition without a proper good-bye, we often find ourselves standing in the same doorway again and again.

As you transition, allow yourself to use all your senses to say good-bye and to savor what was good, while knowing that standing in a doorway, between change, does not all allow for full living.

Although we often do not know what is beyond the doorjamb, completing a good-bye ceremony allows a healthy step into the unknown. We can be afraid of the intense emotions of the good-bye, but feel your emotions with, smiles and tears. Walk through each new period of your life with intention.

January 9

Thoughts
Disordered
Make my
Living uncomfortable, jarred.
Running, I seem
To circle back
To my own disorder.
I sit in stillness
Of unknown.
The white fuzzy
Edges consume
Me
And the
Instability
Requires a new
Balance.

Examining new possibilities at the new year is normal. We often determine that transitions will be painful, and we are not ready, or we are afraid.

Take on one transition at a time to understand the messy process you are entering. Full living with yourself and those you love is a process requiring engagement with messy feelings. Full engagement will mean not knowing at times, feeling like you are not on solid ground.

In the stage of transition, we are unsure and nothing is clear. We have to muddle through this period to make sense of the change. If you are afraid of the unknown and wish everything to be clear all the time, you will be unable to change. Settle into the fuzzy, and let the world clear for your thinking to come into focus.

January 10

Whole generations gone

Leaving only imprints

Names fuzzy but dangling

Family traits continue

Never ready, wondering how

You are

The next generation

To go

Leaving your imprint

And dangling

A piece of your own

Eternity for the

Next generation.

Take time to think about the generation before you, and examine the imprint left to you and your generation. Generations seem endless, but everyone takes a turn at being the generation leaving an imprint.

Within our world, local, and family communities, we leave a piece of ourselves embedded in each of our communities and in the people we come into contact with daily.

Take time to reflect on those who have left an imprint on you, and be thankful for the positive and healthy traits they left to you. Adjust your thinking and habits for the people and communities you wish to affect in the next generation.

January 11

You are in my circle
As intended
Part of a long chain
 Connecting you
To many.
Today I am happy
To have you as part of
My small circle
Knowing you will
Continue the chain
Still linked to me.

There is much to learn from those who are part of your family chain. It is easy to take for granted that the people closest to us will be here forever, but that won't happen.

We are all part of a group of people who have provided us both genetic and learned traits. Over time, the chain of people connected is added to and removed from, each person affecting us and changing the courses of our lives.

Determine what you need to learn from each of those in your history chain. It may be a favorite family recipe, story, or lesson. Reach out to those you call family today to ensure that you are able to keep the links in your chain live productively and that your family is improved from the learning of the elders.

January 12

Paths cross

Some wide and long

Some brief and stunted

But all traveled one step at a time

Differing in impact

Still changing each traveler.

It is important to ensure

The footprints left

Provide light and direction

To each we pass.

We tend to start the day thinking about the tasks needing to be completed or checked off by the end of the day. No task will leave a lasting imprint like helping someone to feel better because you took the time to make a difference in his or her life.

Remember that you leave a legacy that can be positive or negative. Make sure your legacy provides light and direction. Consider your family first, and help make a better day for those you often do not consider. Ensure that the difference you make is not only a benefit to you but focused on another. That is the best imprint of all.

Today, consider making a difference to those you come in contact with at work and in your home. Go out of your way to provide assistance, comfort, and guidance to another.

January 13

Open to warm sunlight

Day begins

Reflection of tasks to complete

Midday adjustments, changing

With the needs

Sunsets fold in the day

And allow for breathing in

Cool evening air and family

Laughter.

Family traditions need to be nurtured. From the morning to the evening, the routines you put in place make a difference to the health of your family.

Examine what your family does to open the day and to close the evening. It is important to open the day with calm and happiness, as the morning sets the stage for the day. Routines that allow for chaos set everyone on a chaotic course for the day.

At the day's end, it is also important to end with harmony and good feelings. One way to accomplish this is around a daily dinner table. Change routines that need to be changed to provide calm and happiness to center your family with positive vibes.

January 14

The young cannot imagine
A body changing
The midlife mirror
Tells a story of an altered
Landscape

Still, living through the miles
Does not help understand
The picture in the mirror
Own the picture
Make adjustments

But love it.

As you age and your body changes, you sometimes can feel like a stranger in your own skin. It is important to stay healthy and fit, but gravity and years will change what healthy looks like. This is the cycle of life.

Wrinkles and brown spots happen. Do not be ashamed or allow them to define who you are and what you are capable of completing. Gray hair and spots of fat happen to all of us.

Change what you can, but don't spend your time worrying about the natural course of each season. Love who you are on the inside and the outside. Do something happy and positive for yourself today.

January 15

Open the day
Smelling fresh cotton
Slowly stretch
With clenched hand
Opening to those sharing
Home
Cat-curl back under
For one more warm-up
Begin anew.

Mornings are special, as each morning starts a new day. Invest in how you start your day, and allow yourself the luxury of being aware of the first light and of the bedding around you.

Think about how you started the morning. This is the time to practice belly breathing and full-body stretches. Allow your brain to visualize the colors of your day, and your voice sending messages to yourself of a good day.

Each day is a cycle in your life for which you get to choose how to respond. You may not be able to control what comes into the day, but you do control how you respond. Spend the first moments of the morning preparing your response.

January 16

Rush, rush

Plates and pots moving

The day requires a filling

From frozen to bubbling

Spoons splatter

Table feels familiar

With people circled

Stop with eye contact

Feel, listen

Fill each heart

With belonging.

Besides the morning stretch, another important routine to examine this month is how we share food with those we love. Are you connected to the people at your table, or are you tapping responses to people outside of the table?

A table surrounded with people is an important place. It provides an opportunity for connection. To fill someone else's tummy and heart is a gift. The dinner table is a place that strengthens the habits of a family.

At your next meal, examine how you are interacting with those around the table, and the of sense of belonging with them. Change the norms by talking about who did what during the day. Laugh, make eye contact, and reach out with a hand of understanding.

January 17

Each shift in nature

Includes an ending

Short, long, happy, painful

But an ending

The end is important, as it

Is a lasting imprint

And defines the beginning.

An in-between time

Allows for gray lines and unknowns,

Then beginning

Blooming and growing

Caution—it's not a straight line.

Understanding the basic nature of change will help you not only examine your own transitions but also better navigate healthy change.

If you seem stuck in a certain spot, you may need to go back and engage in a meaningful ending. Look at it as a ceremony to help you move forward. Or you may be struggling against the in-between period. It is okay to not know every step. This is a perfect opportunity to examine options and reframe thinking. It is a scary place, but beneficial if you use it.

Finally, beginnings bring work, because you are now open to engage in a new path. Be aware that transition is not neat or sequential; understanding its nature will thus help you to navigate change.

January 18

Outside my window

Bare branches

With knobby knuckles

Sway in winter's

Wind

Glistening with morning dew

Slowly breathing

Nature's healing time

To ready for

Rebirth.

We often think of winter as a time when things die, but we can begin to look at winter's hibernation as a time of healing. With days shorter, we can come in from the cold and reflect on the next phase. Winter offers an opportunity for you to reframe your perspectives and determine how you will live from this point forward.

Do not spend time missing the blossoms and green leaves. Spend time shedding your own baggage and getting ready for new growth. Winter is the perfect time to soak in nature's healing power.

This is the time to make your dreams and goals a reality. Think about your heart, and let go of what is keeping you from growing in your next season.

January 19

Season changes
Allow reflection
Heart, mind, body, soul
A year of turning change
Grows us into
Our life-wisdom season
With intention we reflect
Each season's joy
March forward with love.

There are many different kinds of seasons that change. You move from toddler to small child, then to teenager and young adult, each with its own season. Each stage is to be valued for what it brings to your life.

Time marches on, and suddenly, we are the elder generation. Think about each of your seasons and what was positive about each time in your life.

Include daily time for examination of your heart, mind, body, and soul. There can be bitterness with a season change, but daily reflection can change the bitter to the joyful.

January 20

The mountain giant against the sky
Seems eternal
Yet even the mountain is changed
By time
Nature hurls elements of change
Which the mountain gracefully
Allows and accepts.

Acceptance with grace is difficult. You can be certain your rock is in the process of change, as you are always in the process of change. Being able to accept the next cycle with joy is a mindset we all need to work at completing.

There is uncertainty of what will be placed in front of you. Graceful acceptance is not about giving up or not caring but is a healthy reaction to whatever comes into your journey.

Graceful acceptance is about taking a cleansing breath and facing the challenge with a sense of balance and peace to take the next step—even if the step is off the paved road. Be a mountain today.

January 21

Waking to a new morning

A new day

A new season

Grateful to experience

The shift

But the unknown

Frightens

Me

Until I breathe

And allow

The coming unknown.

If it is new, then it is unknown. Some relish the new and unknown, while others can become frozen in fear in the face of it. The one thing certain for all of us is change, and learning to be open to it can help us realize opportunities.

Being grateful and receptive to the experience is a process. Understanding the emotions that the unknown bring forward in you, and the experiences the unknown brings, will help make the new time joyful.

Breathing is essential to life and is essential to bring into the moment of change. Watch how you are breathing today during both happy and stressful moments. Deep belly-breathing will cleanse your body, mind, and spirit and will bring in needed oxygen for solving the new issues that come with new experiences.

January 22

Her own voice tells
Her she is unable
When faced with the new.
Still, she wobbles forward.

Then anger at the fear
Makes her march through,
Sometimes not aware
Of a wonderful journey.

She owns her voice
The words are important
To finally breathe
And face the journey.

With peace and acceptance.

An important cycle to pay close attention to is your self-talk with its patterns. What are you telling yourself at the start of a new season or needed transition? Your own conversation predicts how you will move through your transition.

Examine the words inside your personal conversations. Are the words encouraging, and do they give you permission to change in a healthy way? Do the thoughts provide encouragement?

When you do not encourage yourself, you may find yourself moving through your journey with anger, fighting your way through the path. The right words will help you face a new journey with peace and acceptance.

January 23

Change for her is a challenge
To be studied and analyzed.
Each move is calibrated
And calendared.

But unpredictable and winding
Change does not move within her
Assigned time.

She is now frozen and unsure.
The calculations have not allowed
For finding joy in a surprise.
It is her job to be in the moment.

And uncalibrated.

It is critical that you enjoy your life. If you overanalyze every decision, you can lose precious joy within a moment. Change by its nature is unpredictable. If "plan, plan, plan" is your nature, life is sure to provide a twist.

Unless you accept that things do not always go as planned and are able to be resilient, you will be unhappy and you will miss much of what makes the world enjoyable.

Today, think about how your pattern of planning affects your ability to be present in the now. Does it keep you from enjoying the moment you are in? Do you find yourself planning while you should be engaged in a conversation with a close friend? Balance planning with ensuring that you are in the current moment and able to enjoy it.

January 24

Resiliency is taught

The teacher allows falls and mistakes

In order to teach

Standing again.

The one standing must

Own the mistake

Make amends

Be willing to fail.

The teacher gives the

Next experience with guidance

The one trying to stand again

Must use the wisdom.

Or fall again.

It is important to review our patterns of how we help others. Our patterns of helping other people are personal and change based on the interactions with the people we love. Helping others requires that we teach them to be resilient, and this demands that we allow people to experience failure; the lesson is in how to deal with failure and try again.

The cycle of failure cannot be broken unless we teach how to overcome and move past failure. We teach this lesson by making sure the learner takes responsibility for the errors and then forgives him or herself. Only then is the learner ready to try again.

You may feel you need to protect certain people from their mistakes, but you will deny them of the gift of resiliency if you do so. Examine your patterns of teaching today.

January 25

Listen to your mothers and sisters
Their stories will pave your way
Having visited your path
From many angles
You do not have to repeat
Their tears.

We are connected circles.

Tell your wisdom, mothers and sisters
You have a story that will help
Your wrinkles are paths of knowledge
And have seen many options
You do not have to show, only tell,
Your tears.

We are connected circles.

The connections we have to the women in our lives are very important to examine. Your pattern of interaction may be positive or may be unhealthy.

Think about how you listen to the women around you. What do you pay attention to and what do you discard? The women around you have much to offer from their own experience and from different perspectives. Additionally, you have your own wisdom story to offer to women you know, including the waitress who is waiting for help.

Determine today how to maximize the usefulness of the wisdom of women. Begin to pay attention to what you focus on when you are with the important women in your life. Work to learn from other women and to support all around you.

January 26

She is inside of me
  As I was inside her.
Cord connected,
  Always a fight for
Disconnection.
  Moving my way.
She urges another.
  The cord is shredded
Even rubbed raw.
  It damages both.
Serving life requirements
  She is now gone
But the cord continues
  From somewhere
She accepted inside of me
  And the cord is passed
Inside my own
  Daughters.

The parent-child relationship is delicate and forms much of how we think. It is a connection like no other, but there is also a constant struggle for independence.

Our sons and daughters often feel that they don't want to turn out like their parents. Each of us is a unique and individual person, but we are linked to our family circles. Examine your relationship with your parents or your children. Your pattern of living together or apart can be improved through communication and forgiveness.

As a parent, you may need to forgive yourself; as you know, no parent raises a child perfectly. There are always mistakes. There comes a time when you, as the offspring, recognize that you own your life and mistakes and forgive your parents' past mistakes. We cycle from parent to child, and we choose how the cycle is maintained and adapted.

January 27

Her footstep

Inside mine

His inside hers

We walk together

Tracing our journey

Together

Until her step fills

Mine

And his fills hers.

Grandparents and parents wait for the next generation to emerge. It is important during this waiting period to determine what patterns of living and thinking you wish to pass on in your next chain, your next generation.

Although the steps you have already taken can't be changed, all future steps can be adjusted. Again, think about the steps that you feel are positive and the steps you wish to change so the people following you step in a better direction.

Identify a change in direction and talk with those following you to make sure they know there is a need to change direction. Then complete the change.

January 28

Coloring carefully

Lines inside patterns

Sweating hands

To ensure

No color escapes

The set pattern

Wishing for no

Set boundary

I wish for

Courage.

It takes courage to color outside of the lines. It changes the set ways we have always thought something should be done.

Keeping inside all boundaries stifles thinking and creativity. We all have places in our lives where we want to be free of the lines imposed by others. It only takes one time of moving outside the line to know that it can be done.

Find a place today to dance outside of the lines you have been sweating to stay inside. Be courageous and stop caring what those inside the lines will say. Reflect on how moving outside feels and, determine where else you may step out and be your own person.

January 29

I watch with joy

You become

Part of my circle

With ever-changing

And stretching

To grow

Until you emerge

With your own

Circle of love

While our circles

Continue connecting

You find your

Own space

As it should always

Be.

There is a pattern in how a family grows together. The pattern requires each individual in the family to be transition and stretch in his or her own way.

A family circle will be strengthened by understanding the change process, and by parents and children ensuring that all have their own spaces in which to become the best people they can be.

Today, talk to your family about transitions and change, so they begin understanding the need to maximize their gifts while maintaining the circle of family.

January 30

Place of peace

Body, spirit, and mind

The water

Washes, sprays, cleans

Dark-gray places

Clouding peace

Renewed for

New change.

Learning to create change in your thinking and habits requires a place of calm. That place may be a physical retreat that encourages the cleansing thinking needed for change, but more important, it is a place inside yourself that creates the conditions for renewal.

The space washes away the doubts and concerns that hold us back from taking the action needed for change. It also allows forgiveness for the times when we have strayed far from the path.

When you are able to breathe inside this space, there is a great possibility for productive change. Today, identify space for this kind of thinking, and go to that space regularly for thoughtful reflection and renewal of body, mind, and spirit.

January 31

Cycles, circles, and connections
Define an inner spirit
Acknowledgment
Of each
Deepens understanding
Of self and
The world.
Dependence and independence
Are formed with balance.
Deliberate is the learning
Of how we
Move through
Life.

The patterns of how we think and live are important to improve our lives. The lives of those we are connected to—including those with whom we have close connections and those we touch for only a moment—will be affected by our cycles and patterns.

We can learn from all cycles. The cycle of life, the cycle of nature, and the cycle of thinking can all provide insight into how we can transform ourselves and our world.

At the end of the month in which you reviewed and reflected on your own patterns, it is time to take intentional committed action. Take ownership of your current way of living and persist in becoming a better person.

February

The month of February can put life back into balance after the hectic beginning of the new year. Balance is not continual happiness but a process of shifting the fast-paced world into one in which we focus on centering ourselves with caring about the right amount of challenge and calm in each day.

Balance requires us to listen carefully to ourselves and to our surroundings to follow through on what we say is important to us. Balance is being clear in our thinking by uncluttering our breathing and living.

Balance is always a choice, as is unbalance. When you make the choice for balance, you have decided to work at it each day.

February Focuses

Balance is a choice.

Learn to trust yourself.

Unplug, and learn patience.

February 1

It begins the moment
Life is inside
All encompassing
Giving
A balance of
Protection with independence
Filled with mistakes
No mother does it perfectly
Engaging
A promise of
Commitment with
Free will
To ultimately push
One loved so
Into an unknown
Path
Requiring courage with
Persistence and surrender
There are no answers only giving,
Engaging and loving.

If you want answers to be simple and neat, you will be in constant struggle with a world where answers are always varied and dense. Change, transitions, and improvement are filled with stumbles as we work at our answers.

It is usually the stumble that provides valuable learning, or the situation you most dread that stimulates the opportunity to grow. Face these times with a determined heart and persistence to get to not the one answer but the next right answer, for if you keep examining, you will find more than one right answer, leaving you with possibilities.

Balance the push and pull of life in order to fully engage in living and to balance your questions and answers.

February 2

They are rushing to an end
Looking for the immediate
Not feeling watching or waiting
Just concluding
    They are rushing to an end
    They are rushing to an end
Packing things that
Weigh on their hearts
Technically connected
Wired but unhinged
    They are rushing to an end
    They are rushing to an end
Fighting to be first in line
For the end
Terminally lonely
Calmly, abruptly
    Without path
    They are rushing to an end.

Today, slow down and disconnect. For you to have healthy balance, it is important to feel the air around you. Mind-body-spirit balance requires each of us to stop, watch, listen, and feel the world around us. We need to see the miracle in a spider creating a beautiful web. With everything so immediate and now, today take time to wait, and enjoy the wait time.

We are so connected to phones and internet that we often forget to connect with the people and the world around us. With so much connection, we can be completely disconnected to the person who needs a smile or a hand.

Today, do not rush to an end. Take a walk around where you live, and find a miracle. Take the evening off from the phone, internet, and TV. Listen to the sounds of your house and soak in a peaceful stillness. Wait with joy today and connect with those in your daily life.

February 3

Steady, determined
For those I love
Anchoring those
Hands needing
A place to balance
Themselves
I know
I can be brought
To pieces of
Pebble
If care is not
Taken to
Build and
Energize
My own internal
Rock.

Balancing your own internal struggles while being the rock to others wears at your spirit. If you are a rock for someone or if you have someone who is your rock, take today to reenergize and build what steadies you.

There are often many lights to guide us. If you rely on a single light, it will need to rest at some point, leaving you in the dark. If you are a light to others, help them identify many lights so you can revitalize your own light, for each light must be energized or it becomes weakened.

Find balance between being a light and seeking a light. A person who provides for others is most effective when those he or she shines for are provided many lights. Help identify for others at least one more rock they can use to balance themselves with during times of need. Find an activity that reenergizes you today.

February 4

Corporate rush
Get done, check, check
Drains the body
Depletes the soul
Demoralizes the mind

Draining, depleting, demoralizing
Issues a badge of work honor
And requires a filling of black joe
Into the night
Its own secret abuse

Learning, growing
Demand balance
Rejuvenation
Reconnection
Renewal

Of mind, body, and soul.

There is a scandal in the American workplace every day. You will hear workers saying, "I worked until two in the morning to get this done," or "I haven't spent any time with my family this week." People work this way, thinking it is an honorable way to work, but in truth, it is a disservice to those they work with and those they live with.

We have created a badge of honor for out-of-balance behavior, and it is hurting our country. Workers who are drained, depleted, and demoralized are less creative and less productive. The workforce engages in self-abusive habits that do not develop effective or efficient workplaces. Unfortunately, this imbalance takes the life of many family members too early because of unchecked stress.

Examine and reflect on your own work and determine how you will balance hard work with healthy living. Create work and family boundaries, and stick to ensuring that you spend equal quality time in each place. Rejuvenate, reconnect, and renew both at work and at home.

February 5

In the dimming time

Stretch.

Slow down and put day work away.

Breathe air into your belly.

Shut down the list.

Shoulders, hips, and toes wiggle.

Light recedes.

Healing restoration

Settles into your body

With required

Sleep.

There is day work and night work. During night work, your body repairs and your brain is working to put the world in order. This happens only during the deepest part of the sleep cycle. It does not happen in a cat nap or a short rest, because hours (seven to nine) are needed for this night work to be completed.

Take time to prepare your body and brain for the night work this evening and every evening. Night work requires that the lights go down and computers go off. It is a time to let your body come into comfort.

Your day work should be put away both physically and mentally so you have truly healthy and healing rest. Stop day work with enough time to allow your body to wind down before sleep. Believe in healing and sleep.

February 6

Balanced

Internally centered

Focused

Allows for risk and failure

With a path

Back

Heart beating

For self and others

Ensuring growth

For all.

Balance is a mindset that is worked at each day. When you are balanced, you are focused and able to leverage your potential. Maintaining balance is a practice we all need to engage in from day to day.

To maximize your potential, you need to balance taking risks and sometimes failing with understanding that a balanced person is able to be resilient after failing. Balance allows a person to not focus on the failure but to keep moving toward the growing. It is the art of picking yourself up with grace and understanding that allows growth.

Today, practice being balanced by taking risks and being resilient. Know that finding balance is a practice each day, not something completed in one day. Get to know the feelings when you are balanced, so you can work at repeating that sense of balance.

February 7

Center your courage
Not through other voices
But by listening to the
Interconnected
Beat of your heart and head

Sound is present
But the world's static
Limits listening and
Separates the joint
Voice of heart and head

Centering courage
Focuses on the sounds
Moving inside in order
To begin integrating
Heart, head, and hands.

It takes courage to balance the voice from your head and the voice from your heart. Often, they provide you conflicting information. It takes courage to work to truly connect these two internal voices.

Such connection happens when you listen to both and begin to build trust in balancing your actions with your beliefs. In order to build trust in yourself, you need to stop and listen to yourself rather than the voices of so many other people. When starting this internal conversation, you begin the process of integrating both your feelings and your thinking. It takes courage and time to sort them out and get them in sync.

Today, begin your conversation with your heart and head. Sort out both sides of the conversation and allow yourself a deeper understanding of your internal conversation. It's not easy or simple, but you need to begin the process of balancing your thinking.

February 8

Seek wisdom to come

Inside the center

Of yourself

Find teachers in

Your daily walk

Listen to the lesson

Allow the wisdom

To be contained in your voice

And live the gift

Allowing wisdom to center you.

At the end of each day, you have given your talents and gifts to those around you. Work, family, and friends influence your physical and mental balance. To keep centered and on the right track, connect with those who provide you wisdom.

Using that wisdom will allow you to balance the wear and tear of daily living with a balance between productivity and creativity. You will find these teachers in people who are happy in their work and family lives.

Listen to and watch the behaviors of those who live life to the fullest, and implement their wisdom in your day-to-day living. Find one or two of those teachers to watch and learn from to improve your own balance.

February 9

All I serve take
One piece of me each day,
Gladly given

But guard against
Giving without replenishing
Soul and heart

Giving balanced with taking
Is required by those who serve,
Given gladly.

We serve others every day. We give and continue to give even when we get tired. But giving without replenishing your energy will end with resentment and a loss of self that can hurt everyone.

Work hard at balancing taking from others and allowing yourself to absorb much-needed energy. Balancing both giving and taking might be spending time with a friend or allowing someone to do for you, even when it is uncomfortable. You might even consider having a date with yourself and taking time to browse in your favorite store. Give yourself permission to sit in the park and breathe in a lovely silence. Do not let yourself believe you don't need replenishing.

Reflect today on how well you balance taking and giving. Make an adjustment if you feel they are imbalanced. Listen for words from others and yourself that block you from being able to take from others or from giving yourself time for just you.

February 10

I need *It*

It will solve my unhappiness

When I possess *It*

I will be different

It is there

Within your hand is *It*

It is solid and ready

You will be better with *It*

Understanding *It*

Believing in *It*

Taking hold of *It*

You are the *It*

And it will make you better.

Everyone wants something. It is okay to want things and to work for them. We do need to guard against believing that our lives will be better or that we will be better by getting that one thing we really want.

Realizing that what you need is right inside of you can create a sense of peace. It also can take away the craving for things that you think will make your life better. Changing your attitudes, thinking, and habits give the best chance of give making your life better.

Today, identify your *It* and your external cravings. Gain understanding that you should leverage the gifts you have inside to enable yourself to maximize your potential. The talents you already have are the It. Everyone has talents. Being aware of and acknowledging your talents will help you gain peace and balance.

February 11

Balance is not
Standing without a fall
It is not keeping things
Even

Inner balance
Art and science
Challenging and comforting
Constant change

Balance rides change's
Jarring, turning waves
With one able
To stand again.

Having balance in your life does not mean that everything is smooth sailing. To grow, you must have a mix of challenge and comfort in your life. The ability to balance those shifts from challenge to comfort is the skill to acquire.

If you continually push yourself, you live in stress. Continual stress is unhealthy and eventually makes you unproductive. Keeping things only in your comfort zones does not allow growth and keeps you in a stagnant state.

Inner balance keeps challenge and comfort in line with each other. This balance ensures that you have inner peace, with the ability to stretch and grow. Spend time today reflecting on how you are balancing challenge. Make adjustments if needed.

February 12

Falling and failing
Support inner balance
By nurturing resilience.
Growth
Is the failure
That deepens wisdom.
Using wisdom, we
Balance life.
Cherish failure, as
It is proof that you
Engaged in living.
Learn from the failure.

Fall with grace
And stand again.

Failing is required for living. Balanced people use failing to intentionally build wisdom. Building wisdom happens only when we live without fearing failure and are able to embrace failure as part of learning.

Failure is our teacher for resilience, and the more we practice, the better we are able to stand again and not be defeated by failure. What matters is not how we messed up but how we recover and become better people.

Today, plan what you consider effective steps for bouncing back after something goes wrong. Reflect on how you can use past failures to build your own wisdom bank, and reframe your thinking to consider a past failure as a positive, a wondrous gift.

February 13

Rooms and spaces
Together with
Family foods
Laughter
Quiet reading
Time together
And time alone
Construct
Needed mindset
For living
In harmony.

No matter how big or small your house is, you need to ensure that the rooms and spaces create a feeling of harmony and safe harbor for you and your family.

This can be done by organizing, using color, or even bringing in your favorite scent. It does not need to cost money, but does require thoughtful intention to use your space to encourage living in balance.

Today, adjust one room to make sure you have a place for balancing the outside to make you feel warm, comfortable, and safe.

February 14

Rocks, solid, balancing
One on top of another
Carefully in place

Reminder of the internal
Struggle to keep
Balance in focus

A tumble
Diminishes healthy living
And shifts all balance

Rebuilding anew
Tower of balance
Strong in reminder.

The Native Peoples have clearly understood the importance of balance and used rocks not only to mark direction but also as a reminder of the need to balance internally. Although the rocks are solid, their balance on top of another is fragile.

Rocks can remind us of how fragile a balanced life is and also of how important balance is to our health. The balance you have now can easily shift, but it can also be rebuilt.

Find your own reminder of balance in your life today, and put it in a place that will allow you to see it daily. It should act as a reminder of both how fragile your balance is and of the importance of balance to living fully.

February 15

Green growing plants
Thrive with sun and rain
Accept help to grow
And sprout roots
To support fruits and flowers

Nature's course
Season after season
Previous crops making
Better the soil
For the tiny frail seedlings

Are you balanced for growing?

To continue to grow and develop as a person, you need to make sure that you surround yourself with the right environment. Balance the support and care you give to your body with the nourishment you give to your heart and brain. This will ensure that you are putting yourself in the place of greatest opportunity.

When you make sure that your environment fills you with the ability to thrive, you are balanced for growing. Never discount the environment you are living in; make it a powerful tool for your growth.

Today, take a look at how well your environment allows you to grow. Make one change in your environment today that enriches your body and spirit.

February 16

Colors you see

Inside

Frame thinking

For what is needed next

Internal palette

Listen to your colors

Adjust

Create your own recipe

For peace and cleansing

Of heart

And soul.

You must pay daily attention to what you allow yourself to see and hear inside yourself. Although there is a great deal we do not control, we *do* control our own thinking and self-talk.

It is easy to discount your internal conversations, but those thoughts are continual and affect you each day. You begin and end your day with your internal conversation. The conversation is powerful to the balance or imbalance of your life.

Today, pay close attention to your internal conversations. Are those conversations balanced with challenge and care? If you find one type of conversation overpowering another, work to ensure that both comfort and challenge are part of your daily self-talk.

February 17

She is uneven
When he is sorting
Parts of his life
For change
So connected
The balance
Centers on each
Partner
Balance embedded
In those
We share
Our daily walk.

The people we choose to partner our lives with affect our sense of balance daily with their moods, actions, and improvements. Partner balance is important to individual balance because each type of balance affects the other.

The first step in improving partner balance is to gain understanding of how you help balance your partner and how your partner balances you. Talking with your partner about what keeps you in balance and what causes imbalance will help the partnership.

Today, take time to consider what your partner needs to do to help with your balance and what you can do to help your partner. Then do it.

February 18

Struggling with tears
How did she do it all
Work, home, church
Never done
Tired seeps into bone
Lists without joy
Cross-offs with add-ons
Looking in other windows
She sees others
Effortlessly finishing
Do they do it all and
Finish with nothing?

It's time we begin to understand that no one has it all. There is joy and loss with each decision about how to spend time, but saying, "I have to get it done," is a red flag that we are out of balance.

Everything we have to get done won't bring us joy, but with most of what we do, we need to consider the cost. Getting something done should not mean losing joy.

Lists and "to do's" need to be thought through for real importance. Today, examine your to-do list and ensure that your list does not leave you with feeling nothing. Leave room for experiencing joy each day, and understand that joy is not trying to do it all.

February 19

Wobbling down the sidewalk
Ponytail flying behind her
Determined to master
Peddling and steering
Together
Fall after fall
She asks for one more time
Peddling with persistence
She continues
Working at
Balancing.

Life balance is not something you "get done" but rather a lifetime process of persistence. Just like every six-year-old who is determined to ride a two-wheel bike, you need to be determined to stay balanced in mind, body, and spirit.

You also need to be aware that balancing your life can be an up-and-down process that when rebalancing, life can be a little wobbly. You have to keep trying.

Today, examine an area of your life that you need to work to balance. Don't be concerned if you have attempted the balance before and failed. Remember that balance takes persistence.

February 20

You are your own

A separate individual

Breathing and living to

Your own beat

You are not me

You cannot

Be what I am

Nor can I be you

Our paths have crossed,

Intertwined, and existed

But they do not exist as one,

Because you are you

And I am

Me.

One of the areas of balance important to pay attention to is a sense of self. Many people and tasks take your energy, time, and balance. It is important to maintain a sense of who you are, what you like, and understanding the reasons for who you are and what you like.

Recognizing yourself as a meaningful and valued person is part of maintaining your sense of yourself. Begin to honor your own feelings and desires. Ask yourself, *What do I like, and why do I like it?*

Consider having a "date" with yourself. Do something that you like, and discover why you like it. Allow yourself to be an individual.

February 21

Ringing bells
Welcome all
A family class
Of differences

Ringing bells
Call for many
To grow from
Knowing personal variance

Ringing bells
Publicly include
Making each better
For knowing difference.

Sometimes, we think about balance as getting rid of excess, but we should also think of it as including and interacting with people who are different from our regular circle.

Including people who have different perspectives and ideas can add to your own thinking and can widen your lens. It is an effective way of ensuring that you are balanced. It also keeps you learning.

Today, reflect on how you are including not only people like you but also people different from you. Take time to have a conversation with one of those people who have a different perspective; listen rather than defend, and reflect on how that person's perspective helps you balance your own.

February 22

Balancing begins
With the earth
We stand on,
Ensuring we have
Taken
What is needed
And giving
Back
What is needed
To renew.
It is balancing
Our own spot
On earth to
Sustain our
Own deep
Breathing.

Every person has a responsibility to balance his or her patch of earth. Critical for each person to be internally balanced is the balance of his or her environment.

Take one step to balance your own spot of earth. Maybe start composting, or start carpooling one day a week. When we leave a smaller footprint on this earth, we make a difference.

Today, take one step toward balancing your spot in your neighborhood or community. Find one way to make a difference, and stick to it. Make a commitment to giving back to the earth.

February 23

Power, internal force
Provides the presence
To heal self
And others.
Force and energy
Must be
Acknowledged
And honored,
As the choice
To use your
Power
Creates space for
All spirits
To grow.

Internal power is positive. We often shy away from using our own power. Perhaps we fear that it makes us aggressive or worry that others will label us, but power is positive, and we need to learn to balance our power in our daily living.

We can use power to heal ourselves and those we encounter each day, but in order to heal, we need to acknowledge and honor our own power. Power is integrated into our words and actions.

Examine your power and determine how you might begin to use it for positive change for yourself and others. How are you thinking about your own power? Are you seeing yourself as powerful? Take a turn at using your positive power.

February 24

A woman's voice

Complex, cautious, confident,

Is taught to be

For others

But exists

To guide

Her own path

Balance

Your voice to

Stretch and protect.

The words you have with yourself may be the most important conversations you have. You want to make sure that your own words are balanced with encouragement and restraint. This allows risk and caution to move you forward and protect you from unnecessary hurt.

Your voice is complex, so you need to pay attention to all of your thinking and talking. This requires you to be intentionally aware of what you are saying inside your head and to redirect when necessary.

Today, keep a short journal of your words and identify your conversations as positive and negative. Determine what topics you need to redirect, and create a plan to make those changes.

February 25

Filling heart and soul,

As important as

Breathing

Of joy,

Requires you knowing

What joy

Means to

You.

Life is busy and rushed. We tend to try to take care of everything for everybody. In the busy rush of life, we forget to fill our own hearts and souls, and we lose the meaning of joy.

Being on the treadmill without feeling joy is dangerous for yourself and your family. Step off periodically to refill. Ask yourself, *Do I know what joy is to me?* You have to know yourself and what you like in order to have true balance.

Today, step off for a little while and do something simple that gives you joy. Maybe it is a walk during lunch or a stop off at your favorite browsing store. Know that finding joy for yourself is a gift to your family.

February 26

You heard my voice

Inside a watery womb.

It guided you

Through walking, running, stumbling.

Balance my voice

With your own.

Listen to both

But trust the voice

Developed by your experience.

I do.

Balancing your voice with those of the people who love you is often difficult. You can feel that you are not being respectful when you go against their advice. You can even feel resentful when the voices don't meld. You can hear the voices of those you love and discount your own voice.

Try instead to listen and hear both those you love and yourself. After listening to both, don't be afraid to trust your decisions. Even when there is disagreement, trust your own voice.

Think about a recent difficult decision and determine the voice you heard and the decision you made. Were you listening to yourself? Are you able to trust your own voice? Work at listening and trusting yourself.

February 27

Airplane arms

Believe you can fly

Feet running

For air and lift

But solid on ground

You turn

And elevate

Your ideas

Into the world.

Do you remember playing airplane on a windy day and being sure you would be lifted to fly? Balancing believing with keeping your feet grounded is a tricky endeavor—an endeavor we all need to try.

It is important that you put your ideas into action in a logical and thoughtful manner without fearing failure to lift off. The fear can dismantle any idea.

Reflect on something you have wanted to complete, but have talked yourself out of doing. Think about what the first step might be to complete your idea, and then do the first step. Keep at it, step by step, until you implement your idea.

February 28

Balance is

Work always

In process,

A continual struggle and joy

For heart and brain.

Equilibrium

In choices for

Challenge and comfort.

This is life's

Ebb and flow.

Balance happens only

By choice.

This month was a reflection on balancing mind, body, spirit, and earth. The most important idea to remember is that balance is something you do every day, and you have to work at it continually.

The fortunate thing about balance is that it is a choice, and if for some reason, you did not choose it today, you can choose it tomorrow. Although balance is a struggle, it is also a work of joy.

Choose to work at being balanced. Reflect on your choices about balance. What behaviors indicate that you are currently in balance? Take steps to practice balance by ensuring that all the areas of your life are being nourished.

March

Family is a complicated jumble of individuals drawn together by blood lines and choices. Our families can be joyful and painful in the same moment. Positively connected families *work* on connections, inclusion, and forgiveness.

Taking time to reflect on our various family connections and rituals strengthens our own understanding of our complicated relationships. The many habits and rituals from our family are what guide and frame our daily thinking as well as our habits.

Use this month to think about how you interact with those you love and call family. To strengthen the bonds of family, we can begin the conversations and actions needed to improve the potential those we love and call family.

March Focuses

Celebration of connection.

Inclusion of all.

Forgiving to strengthen.

March 1

Smaller than

A pea

But perfectly

Formed inside a

Cushion of life.

We watched you grow

From the outside.

Filling her

Space, you grew

Fingers and toes.

We long to

Cushion

Your journey

With love.

Growing is a beautiful cycle that begins with the words "you're pregnant." When you bring a life into this world, it is a magical period and should be a joyful time.

There is a chain of family members watching and waiting for the next link in the chain to emerge. It is important during this time to determine what patterns of living and thinking you wish to embed in this new person.

Bringing a new family member into your family circle is wonderful. Work to ensure that every person knows he or she is accepted and loved by the entire family. Your words and touch matter in the journey of growing together.

March 2

They rub their bellies,
Unconscious
Of the nurturing already
Beginning.
Nine months
Of an
Amazing growth journey
For mother and
Baby.
Time well spent
For both
Develops mind, body, spirit
In tandem,
A routine to be
Repeated
In all phases
Of life.

The time while mother and baby share a heart and body is the miraculous beginning of a life journey. It is a time for mother and baby to be fully aware of one another, a time to develop not only fingers and toes but also a parent's mind.

A parent's mind not only begins to keep track of tennis shoes but also intuitively understands a struggle or a heartbreak. Even with intuitive understanding, there is much learning for a parent to begin to develop.

This is only the beginning of the transition into a lifetime of guiding another human through life's trials and tribulations. The support the mother provides is continued in all phases of life, until the baby intuitively cares for the parent. Develop your parent's mind for all those you care for in your daily life.

March 3

She wants

To fill her

Womb and life

With a miracle.

She waits

And wonders

For the change

In her body

And the continuation

Of her being.

There are many different ways to fill our world with miracles and to build a lasting impression. As you go through your day today, take time to reflect on what miracles you are part of in your daily life, and how you ensure that those miracles are continued.

People believe that miracles are larger-than-life events, but the truth about miracles is that they can be anything that makes a difference in someone's life or thinking. The miracle of relationship is engaging and affecting another life.

Today, think about that special family member who needs your miracle, and how you can help that person. It may be asking the right questions to help him or her think through a situation, or posing a challenge to improve a current situation. Then ponder how you will help that person continue after you are not there to offer support.

March 4

My father's hands look like art
Black dirt in his creases, stubbed,
craggy fingers, a callus worked in
by his ring

Like a soft canvas edged in by a
knife.

But those hands worked a craft
Mended knees from fallen bikes,
understanding touches,

Like the sea cradling abundant life.

I love his hands. They scratch my
skin but feel sensitive and tender,

Like his craft.

My father worked magic with his
hands. There is much we can do
with our own hands for those in
our family. Taking time to touch a
person in passing or holding a
hand of someone needing care is a
touch of healing.

Have you taken notice of how
often you reach out to touch those
you live with and those that you
love? The touch of those we love
can be calming and add the
feeling of belonging.

Today make a special effort to give
that touch that is unexpected and
watch the faces and body
language of those you love. Use
the craft of touch to make
someone's day.

March 5

It wasn't because

You were good

Or because

You were bad,

And not because

You were just there.

There was no reason

And I can't tell you

Why

It just happened.

Some things happen in a family and there is no one to blame; they just happen. The things that happen in the course of a family's life are not as important as what family members do after they have happened.

Whether the event is a death in the family or dissolution of the current family structure, how we react and what we do moving forward matters. Our reactions and actions matter but can also be amended at any time. Understanding that some things just happen and accepting that they happened can free us to react positively.

We can decide to positively adjust our actions. Today, reflect on a situation to which you can choose to positively adjust your actions. Only you own your actions, and you can choose today.

March 6

Home building,

Balanced lines

And colors,

Creating harbors

And shells

For those I

Call in.

The physical peace

Must match

The emotional and

Spiritual

Spaces within.

Balance and create

With me

The shell

The harbor

The home.

It is important to create places of safety within your home as harbors for yourself and your family. Creating such a harbor may mean finding space or changing a space with things that give you physical, emotional, and spiritual peace.

Understanding the impact that the spaces within your home have on you and your family is important. Creating a safe harbor may require clearing clutter, or making sure the kitchen table is able to fit all for dinner.

Take a look at your home and decide what you may be able to strengthen to create your own harbor. Make those small changes, and watch the effect on the physical, emotional, and spiritual peace of those you call in to your home.

March 7

A life's tapestry
Each stitch important
Coloring a life story
Some stitches skipped
Some perfectly inset
All tell the tale
Of perfect imperfection
All leave unfinished
Work
With stitches needing
Completion
Stitches left
For those we love
To finish
Our final story.

We all leave unfinished business in this world. The people we love need to have the comfort that their work will be continued and finished. To complete their work, you need to know their stories and what is important to finish.

This requires conversation and observation with all family members. What is their work? What are their joys? Finding out what they believe is important to their lives is critical. This should not be a dreaded conversation but one that allows a better understanding of who your family member is and what his or her legacy is.

Today, find out from one person in your family what is important to him or her, and value that with words and actions. Let this family member know that his or her work is important to you and is part of your family legacy.

March 8

Smiling eyes
See familiar
Foods, fun, folktales
With family,
Practiced and passed
From one circle
To the next,
Allowing a new
Set of smiles
To continue.

Families need to create lasting rituals that are familiar to all. Meals around the table, laughter about family silliness, and stories about those we love are important to the rituals.

Review how your family is using its rituals to bond all of you together. Time together is critical to making and strengthening your rituals. Family rituals are an ongoing happening.

Think about one of the rituals you and your family most enjoy, and about one that you might want to create. Make plans to strengthen an existing family ritual around food, fun, folktales.

March 9

Passing years
With stories
And code words.
All families have their own.
Some provide laughter
To insiders only.
Some need
Forgiveness and freeing.
All families
Hold both laughter
And forgiveness.

Today, find a moment to share part of your family story with your youngest member. While all families have tales good and bad, our stories are meaningful to those wondering how they are connected.

Your family history is an important teaching tool, so use it to help others improve their thinking and capabilities for living full and engaged lives. It is important to share our stories both of struggle and happiness.

Pick your stories—perhaps one of struggle and one of laughter—and tell them to that person in the family you think most needs a family history boost.

March 10

Plates filled

Rules to eat

Father sits

In watch

Chewing and chewing

Liver

Panicked

Waiting

To cough

Depositing liver

To trash

Father knows.

Meal sharing is an important family time. One common family rule is to clean your plate, and on those nights when my mother cooked liver, my parents kept the conversation going while we kids chewed away.

Positive conversation during a meal is a key to a positive family environment. Create that climate by making sure that electronics are not part of dinner time, and plan positive conversation. Having each person in charge of a conversation starter for the meal is a good way to get positive conversation in your family meals.

Today, plan your next set of meals to get your family started on positive family time. Make sure the family is connected to one another rather than to technology. Just don't cook liver.

March 11

Words only enter

When it hurts.

Then words

Tumble out in

A rush,

Seizing the

Emotions that

Are always

In check.

So raging

Are the words.

Silence is safe.

Words are very important in each family. We seem to allow our hurtful words to tumble out. Words we would never say to a friend, coworker, or even stranger, we will say to those who love us most— our family.

Words said in just a few seconds can hurt for a lifetime. Equally, silence produces a difference kind of hurt that stings for a lifetime. What we say and how we treat our family matters.

This month, with family as a focus, take care to watch your words and your silence. Plan your words to heal, and end silences with understanding. Today, pick one person you will change with your words.

March 12

Complicated and scary
She formed
Many parts of me
But she pushed a
Drive in me
To succeed
And a courage
To defy
Even someone
So scary
To walk my own path.

Parent-child relationships can be the most loving and the most complicated. The balance between nurturing and challenging those closest to us is difficult for all parents. It often can result in a relationship that is strained.

As a child, take a look at your own parents and forgive the unbalanced moments in your life. If you are a parent, forgive yourself for those moments.

Parenthood is hard, and it is easy to be critical of yourself. As you walk your own path, take a moment today to thank those who took the time to be parents to you. Pick up the phone and give them words of gratitude.

March 13

Sunday dinner
Table's set
All join
Together
Loud, jumbled,
Organized mess.
Week's tidbits
Bad joke
All laugh,
Pushing away.
Dishes for 10.
Soap and smiles.

Time with family is the most precious gift we have and should be treasured. It requires work and can easily be put off for another day. Every day we get together as a family, our family grows. Family is loud, messy, and wonderful.

Planning time together and relaxing despite your the jumble of schedules will bring your family together. The time together doesn't have to be Sunday dinner, but it needs to be time when you come together to share your lives.

Make a date for your family this week and see if you can continue with some time each week. Although the time won't be perfect, your family members will come if there is laughter.

March 14

Conflict,

A fear of

Losing something

Unnamed and untouchable.

A safer path,

Building anger inside.

Understand

It can be unleashed.

The unnamed something

Is scary.

Words can slash away at

Loving you.

Family conflict is part of living. It is critical that we teach others and practice how to have conflict. We are most comfortable with those we love and are at ease with saying the harshest words to those we value.

Words said in anger are often finished with "I am sorry" or "I did not mean it," but the words leave emotional scars that are always present and easily renewed.

Be determined to teach rules for family conflict. Make sure that everyone in your family knows the danger of harsh words. Find a way today to talk about past harsh words to someone in your family to start the healing.

March 15

It's complicated

A life of

Success and failure

Creating individual

Views of the world

Trying to find

The lens we can share

And the conversation

That will

Help improve

The view.

A family is a connected group of individuals with varied opinions, ideas, and lifestyles. It is complicated to keep family members integrated while honoring individuals.

Each family member is unique and carries an individual set of values, memories, and views. Allowing those individual parts of each person requires patience and perseverance.

Today, honor another family member's values, memories, and views by letting that person know you understand that his or her differences bring value to your family. It is okay for family members to hold those differences. The differences make a family stronger when they are honored.

March 16

Failing is

A mother's gift

Of learning.

Failing

Is easy.

Standing, facing, wobbling

Are hard.

Allowing

The fall,

Visionary

To teaching

Standing again.

Framing failure as an opportunity is perhaps the best gift you can give to child. While it is important to focus on positives and to guide our children to success, it is equally important to allow failure. Failure builds resiliency and allows practice in recovery.

Little failures are easier than big failures to teach the skills of resilient recovery. It is often said that we learn more from failing than from succeeding, so ensure that those you love have the opportunity to learn.

If you have been keeping someone from failing, begin your teaching with a conversation. Let her or him know it is time for wobbling and that a fail is not the end of the world but not knowing how to stand again is.

March 17

Common ground

A line of eyes

All with

A fleck of

Familiar

Different

And the same

Family

Connects and continues.

Have you celebrated your family nose or the special color in everyone's eyes? The same color found in your father's eyes? The laugh belonging to your family that is recognized at family gatherings?

Finding and celebrating those special traits in your family is important and values your family connection. Each family has special and unique characteristics that can be celebrated only inside the family.

Today, take time to first value your own shared traits and then give a call to a person who shares your trait. Let that person know that you love sharing a family trait with him or her.

March 18

I wish you
The freedom
To fly to
The places
In your
Heart
I wish you
The courage
To land
And explore
Each wonderful
Stop in
Your journey
I wish you
The peace
To be able
To see
Yourself
Through each
Adventure.

We all have to travel paths unknown to others. Blessing your family members with the freedom to find their own ways also provides them a path back to the family and keeps connections open.

Even when a family member's adventure isn't one you would take on for yourself or when you think it might be a mistake, giving trust to that person you love to take an unknown path is a gift. When you give trust, you also give the blessing of allowing the journey without the words "I told you so."

If you have someone wanting your blessing, give it. Provide your pros and cons and then support the choice the person makes. Even if the journey does not work out, it will provide an opportunity for learning.

March 19

Weight

Balanced on her

Head

Responsible

Reliable

Rebelling

Two under wing

She worries

It won't be right

A mistake

And she will lose

Love and her own care

Weight.

Different people carry the weight of caring for family at different times. If you have carried responsibility for siblings or for family members, you can feel alone.

Family responsibility needs to be shared. It may be that you need to give up the control of the weight, which means someone else will take it on in his or her own way. That person may not take that weight on in the way you would, and that is okay.

Take steps today to recognize those who feel the weight, and help them let it go or at least release some of the pressure. Think of one or two strategies to help the person feeling the weight of caring to understand that it is shared.

March 20

Stranger without

Family traditions

Enters with a hole in

The circle

He cautiously wanders in

And builds love

With patience

Understanding each member

The circle changed

Accepted member

With traditions

Fine-tuned.

Family structures are blended and revised, meaning we have new people coming into our family circles. It can be difficult for a new member of the circle to navigate when he or she doesn't understand the family code.

It takes time, patience, and understanding for your family circle to include the new son-in-law, parent, or friend, but those on the inside can smooth the way.

If you have a new family member, take him or her aside to share a family story that provides a better lens to the inside circle. Help him or her with time, patience, and understanding to join your family circle.

March 21

Mixed opposites

Find sharing

Life

In small spaces

Give way to

Larger fears

Polite words

Until space moves in,

And people

Must mesh

Into

Aligned counterparts,

Waiting to love.

A family is a group of individuals who have not only similarities but also differences in opinions, lifestyles, and feelings. Sometimes these differences can create separation and hurt.

Our differences do not need to create separation or hurt but can create a stronger bond and feelings of acceptance. This is what positive families do with differences.

Today, have a conversation with your family about what makes each of you different. Guide the conversation to help each family member know that the differences are appreciated.

March 22

Dissolving a family
Tears and scars
Leaving marks on each
Rearranging a family
To function
Care, and continue
Members adjust
To new connections
And define family
Anew.

It is difficult to reframe how we go about rearranging and restructuring how we live as a family. The need to redesign family arises while we are in pain, but rearranging allows for family to be redefined rather than dissolved.

When we can work to continue to care about those in our families during difficult times, we have the chance to redefine and restructure our families. Working and caring about our family allows the family stories to stay intact and for members to continue a relationship, although that relationship may be altered.

If you have a family needing to restructure, help your family members with small steps. Start with a conversation with the children, letting them know that families can look different and still honor what was. Relationships can change, but caring can continue.

March 23

Born to another

Yet sharing my heart

Two young men

Join my family.

Shaking heads

They wonder at the

Laughter around the table

But smile.

Their differences

Make us stronger

And we know

We belong.

I have two son-in-laws who came to our family within the past several years. Both wonderful young men are able to make my daughters happy. They needed to find ways to find their places and integrate into our family.

A family needs to be open to a newcomer's differences, and supportive of efforts to integrate into the family. Each person takes a different path and his or her own time to integrate. We all have people who join different circles, and we all can find ways to be open to the strengths they bring to the group.

Celebrate the differences of all those in your family. Both new and veteran members will be happy to know the strengths that all bring to the family.

March 24

Shoes in a line
Big to small
Footsteps
Taken
Footsteps
Waiting
Muddied, lost
And found
New and shiny
Old and worn
Shoes in a line
Tell our story.

Today, take time to take stock and have gratitude for the shoes in your line. All the shoes will have their own personality and wear and tear on their soles, but all bring value to the family.

The gratitude for the uniqueness of each pair will be noticed and appreciated. It is important that members of the family are able to feel that while they are in a line, each brings something special to that line.

Today, really look at what is unique and positive about each of the members of your family. Then find a special way to let them know about what you found. You might let them know with a phone call or a card, but make the connection.

March 25

He knows every

Crying spot

And angry place.

He stops there

Occasionally,

But one has his smile.

Another looks at the world like him.

Both have a world of pictures

Containing him.

He is honored

As father—gift giver.

The father of my children is a wonderful father. He gave my two daughters a rich heritage as well as his humor, his nose, and a special way of looking at the world.

With my girls sharing so much from their dad, valuing him is easy. Even though he and I lost our way as a couple, we restructured how our family worked. We put the girls first, and it allowed them to feel a connected family.

If you are separated, have restructured your family, or are currently struggling with your child's other parent, find a way to honor them in order to honor your own children with what they share: their parents.

March 26

Conceived and carried
They march forward
Strong
Always told
"I am here."
If they listen
Hard,
They will
Hear my words
And heart
In their own
Children.

The messages you provide to your children are heard and internalized. Every parent wants to make sure those messages are positive because their children carry these messages forever.

An important message for all children to hear is that they are loved. We want to make sure that when it comes time for them to make those hard life decisions, they hear "Do the right thing," even when we are not with them.

Today, reflect on the messages your own children are carrying. If you need to change the messages, start today to provide the message you want them to hear. If the messages are already positive, strengthen them. Make sure that your children know they can hear your message even when you are not there, if they will only listen.

March 27

Two late entries
Amaze my filled heart
Changing my name
Forever
I feel
Unexplainable Love
Known only to
Those
Seeing a new
Generation
Come into life.

Becoming a grandmother is a life-changer. The feelings are so very strong when you hold your grandchild for the first time. But whether we are grandparents, parents, or simply people wanting to make a difference in the next generation, we all need to do our part to raise the next generation.

Making a difference in the next generation requires a commitment to spending time and sharing skills, wisdom, and laughter with them. We all need to give to the children, the next generation, to improve our current world.

Today, have that conversation with a small person. Spend time with your grandchild or a child who needs a hand or an ear. Be a voice for children in your village.

March 28

Circle closed

Formed inside of me

They now say

Words

With my tone and eye roll

Words and actions

They once disdained

Proving we

Are

Circle closed.

Our children in many ways follow our lead, sometimes even when they don't want to follow. Our children work to separate from us. We may hear "I don't want to be you" from them, but in their thirties, they find themselves doing and saying things that are just like us.

If you have children who are in the years when they have to separate from you, understand that it is hard work to separate from the person who gave you life. There is life after separation.

Today, take time to help your children understand separation, and make their work easier by not taking the separation personally. If your children have gone through the separation, celebrate the ways they are different from you as well as the habits and thinking you share.

March 29

Fragile strength
Works to band
Together
People connected
By a life cord
And a lifetime
Of stories.
Protect and guard
The strength
And pass it forward.

Human beings are fragile, even the strongest among us. The connections we have in our families are also fragile. Those connections need to be guarded and cared for every day.

The links we have are strengthened by our shared experiences and by growing together as a family. The family ties can be passed from one generation to the next, along with the ways to maintain the fragile bonds.

Today, recognize how fragile your family is and let your family know how you will protect and guard your own family. Let each person know how important it is for everyone to take care of family.

March 30

Those without

Are easily included

To become part of our stories

Some keep our path

Others are cared for

And then take another path

But leave with

Knowing

Family.

Many people, through a variety of circumstances, do not have families of their own. Including others into your family circle is kind and healthy for the family. It demonstrates acceptance and brings differences into the family.

When you are able to include someone at Christmas or just for Sunday dinner, you demonstrate love and care for a bigger picture to the younger members in the family.

Not everyone will stay forever, but they can be better people because they interacted with your family, and your family will be better for spending time with and learning to love others.

March 31

Family

Quirky Strange, Funny

Tolerant Inclusive, Accepting

Of habits, words, and deeds.

A group different

From others.

Varied from inside

Tied by a single beating heart.

Striving to develop individuals

And stay banded together

Causes conflict and

Untold hurts.

Family

Quirky Strange, Funny

Tolerant Inclusive, Accepting
Strengthens with understanding

All it is.

Family needs to be celebrated, cherished, and connected. It is good that we spend a month in thoughtful reflection about the people that mean the most to us.

While we are a connected group, each individual needs to be allowed his or her unique characteristics, and those characteristics should be honored. The more the individual can be valued, the more each can bring value to the family.

Families are all different and have different needs—needs requiring daily thought and work. Understanding each other and the family unit helps us create a better world.

April

The month of April is a great time to reflect on choice. There is great power and freedom in realizing that you have the ability to choose for yourself. The freedom and power of choice come with accepting responsibility and a great deal of work.

Most of the choices we make in our lives and each day come with the requirement of work. You don't just choose to be a college graduate; you choose to accept the work required to be a college graduate. Just as you choose the work you do, you choose the people you allow to influence you. Understanding choice provides you with the power to change your life.

As you reflect this month on your own choices, make a positive decision to strengthen the good choices and redirect the choices that create hurt or chaos in your life.

April Focuses

Choosing positive power.

Choosing paths.

Owning our choices.

April 1

Paths entered,

Crossed

Without wandering,

But intentionally,

With

Purpose.

The paths

Are chosen

Even with mistakes,

The paths are

Mine

To take.

Each of us is on his or her own journey. Make no mistake, you determine what you make of the paths you take. You may not be able to choose every journey you take, but you can determine how you react and what you allow to affect you along the way.

You can make decisions with intention rather than wandering through life without a determined direction. It is important that you know you have the power to change your path. The mistakes we make affect our life but do not need to define who we are.

Today, take a look at your current journey, and determine what choices you are able to adjust. How are you reacting to the positives and challenges, and what you are allowing to affect you? Choose one thing you can change, and make the decision to create a positive effect on your daily life.

April 2

A thought
Of school bells
Laughing
Sharing small secrets
Acting and engaging
In meaningful work
Helping
Allowing others to grow
A choice
Of living joy
Blessing
And taking
The right choice.

Every day, we need to reflect on and determine how our thinking, actions, and choices affect others. We can bring heartbreak and hurt, or we can bring healing and happiness.

Whatever our work is, we can make it meaningful by positively affecting others. Helping others may be as simple as asking how someone is and then stopping to listen to the answer.

Today, choose to find several ways to allow others to grow through your good decisions. Let others see and experience your joy in choosing your working and living.

April 3

Each person
Makes choices
From a place
Known only to them.
While others
Have played into
The decisions,
Final choices
Are owned
By one
From a place
Adapted and accepted
By one.

It is important that we take ownership of our choices. Often, the choices we make do not affect our lives right away, but eventually, they do make an impact. We tend to want to blame and find fault with anything and anyone other than ourselves.

The truth of why we might not have the job we want may be because of our previous choices. It may be easy to blame teachers or parents, but it is wiser to own our own choices and then do something about them.

Doing something about the decisions and choices we have made is the key. It is also the harder road. Take today to determine a past choice you would like to do something about, and create a plan of action to correct course.

April 4

My internal
Light shines
With its own
Power
I am sure
It is here to
Act in my life
And others'
Positively
And
Powerfully.

Recognizing your own internal light and feeding it power is the first step in choosing how to shine your light for others. Positive power is an essential part of living in peace with yourself and others.

Quiet meditation is a method of internally feeding your own light. Only a few moments daily are required to breathe deeply and energize your own light. The more you are able to calm your thoughts and emotions, the more power you have for yourself and others.

Today, find time in your busy day to sit still and turn inside for a few moments. With your eyes closed, use your words and thoughts to energize your positive power. Then shine for others.

April 5

A lens

Providing a clearer

Picture

Choosing the lens to

Help you view

Your world

The picture

With the glass

Of a single

Lens

Shows only

A single

Choice

Change your

Lens

To see

All possibility.

We can be sure there are many lenses to view the world from each day. A change in the lens you choose can bring clarity or can make your very clear picture blurry. To see the whole picture of the world, never use only one way to look at what is around you.

You change the lens by first understanding that there is not just one right picture but many pictures that may be right. Your conversations with those who don't share your lens is a start to new viewing.

Today, be open to new lenses by not finding fault with a new way to look at an issue or view. Allow yourself to explore the new perspective with curiosity.

April 6

I am not your doll,
A pretty thing
Left for you to
Dress and undress
At your leisure.
I am not your doll,
With a bobbing head
Whose eyes open
And shut on command
For you.
I am not your doll,
With an ever-present smile
Painted across
My face
To comfort you.
I am not your doll.
I did not come
From a box.
I will not go
Into a Box.
I am no one's doll.

Fairy tales and princess stories can leave girls with passive perception of who they are and what their choices in life are. Once girls understand that we all have choice, no one can force them to be someone else's dolls.

There is great power in gaining the knowledge that you have a choice about who you are and how you will live your life. This knowledge is balanced by the understanding that all choices require giving up certain things in order for dreams to become a reality. Balancing your choices is not easy.

Today, reexamine where you are passive in living your life, and determine if being passive is your decision. If it is, give up any anger you may feel, because you have decided that this is your path. If you cannot give up the anger, it may be time to choose a new path. Weigh your choices, and take the power to decide your new path.

April 7

Fearful is the
Struggle and
The problem
Until
Turned
And developed
As a
Waiting
Opportunity.

There is a wonderful thing about choice: you can choose how you approach a problem. Problems are scary until you choose to see them as new opportunities.

Viewing a problem as an opportunity requires you to take a step back and reexamine the issue. Reframing a problem will take logic and analytical thinking, along with strong creativity—a powerful method of thinking that must be nurtured.

Today, choose one of the family or work issues you have been dealing with to use dual thinking with. Use your logic to deeply understand the issue without an emotional edge, and then use your creativity not to solve the issue but to view it as an opportunity.

April 8

Boxes and boxes
Rows of neatly
Organized pieces
Of your life.
I suffocate inside
A put-away box,
Waiting until
You deem me
Suitable or desirable
To your needs.
I am
Unseen
Unheard
Unhappy
In your
Rows and rows
Of neatly organized
Boxes.

No one belongs in a box, and only one person can put you there: you. Exercise your personal power to be free, and determine how you interact with others. You give others the power to affect you or take away their ability to influence you. It is your decision.

It is important to review those whom you allow to influence you. You choose those people and allow the influence. If the people currently influencing you are positive, open yourself to their influence. If they are negatively affecting you, discontinue their influence.

Today, examine your influences and ignite your own power to decide who will influence you. Make the changes today in how your use your power.

April 9

I choose my

Work.

While tasks

Must be accomplished,

My work

Creates

Meaning

Opportunity

And Hope

For those

Around me.

My choice

Is contentment

Of work.

Fortunate are those who love the work that pays their way. Although in every line of work, some tasks have to be completed that are not enjoyed along the way, loving what you do is a joy. There is always opportunity in your day to engage in what you love.

You can create meaning in your work if you really understand what gives you meaning. It might be making a connection with coworkers and giving them organizational or personal hope. It may be about providing your expertise so their work is easier.

Today, determine what gives you daily meaning, and infuse what has meaning for you into your work. Having meaning at work makes the difference between simply going to work and creating a meaningful life.

April 10

She dances

With only a

Shadow

Covering

Dimming

Darkening

Her very

Light.

She will

Continue

To shadow dance

Until she

Allows

Her light

To shine

Through the

Shadow.

If you are not living to your full potential, what decisions have you made to allow your potential to be shadowed? You own your potential, and with work, you can bring it to full capacity.

Everyone, even the most confident person, has areas of potential not completely fulfilled. We need to put ourselves into the right place for our potential to grow.

Today, shine a light on your potential. Determine what might be holding you back, and create a plan with small doable steps for the week to begin to put yourself in a place where you grow your potential.

April 11

Chasing and running
Path to path
To find a perfect fit.
Tired, I slow.
No path seems a fit
Until,
Step by step
The love
Of the imperfect
Path
Sets me on my
Journey.

Looking for the perfect fit and for everything to be just right is one way to sidestep the right choice. The right choice almost always requires us to work at it. The right choice is almost never the easy one.

Learning to anticipate the imperfect, even finding joy and opportunity in the imperfect, is one way to embrace the right choice. Taking time to examine and analyze the issues in your path and determining how to work through them is part of the perfect journey.

When you have a choice that does not feel "perfect," take time to determine the issues and what work may be needed for you to continue on rather than jumping to the next path. When we jump, we often lose valuable lessons and possibilities.

April 12

He wanders,

Lingering

Through

Me,

Stretching,

Moving,

Shaping

Me.

When

He is

Through

Lingering,

I wonder

What I

Will

Feel.

The people we know and relationships we have with them affect our paths, but we control who we allow to pass through our lives, and what to what degree of freedom they have to influence our spirit and thinking. We have to understand that we control who we let into our personal space.

This may be one of the most difficult choices we have in our lives. Sometimes the people whose access to our personal space we need to limit are people we love or who provide a comfort of some kind to us, even though they are negative influences.

Today, take time to examine both your positive and challenging relationships. We all have challenging relationships, so choose one you find especially challenging and begin to redefine its limits. Start with the amount of time you will spend with this person, and keep notes on how the change affects you.

April 13

Morning choices
Stretch into the day.
Unsure of what will
Find me,
I know I alone
Find
My spirit
Of mind.

Every morning provides a new set of choices and the capacity to accept the work needed to realize your dreams. To make our hopes become reality, each of us alone needs to focus mind, body, and spirit to complete the work needed to move toward the goal.

Only so much work can be done in this twenty-four-hour period; the remaining work can get done tomorrow. Finding and focusing your mind, body, and spirit on the right work can help you accomplish great things.

Where ever you are in your day, stop and close your eyes to focus and center your attitude on today's tasks needing to be done to bring your hopes and dreams to a reality. Create a reminder to focus your mind, body, and spirit for each day.

April 14

It is a place where I am alone,
And it feels good.
I can shut the door
And begin to know who I am.
I am happy there
Because it is a place
Where I am free to be
Myself—
My own mind.

Often, we make choices in a fast-paced life without knowing our own minds. Daily thinking and meditation to know yourself and listen to your own voice with confidence is essential. You cannot make good decisions if you do not know what you want rather than what is easy.

It is easy to get lost in the daily grind and to wake up not knowing who you are or what you like. Using even just five minutes each day to quietly listening to your own thoughts can help you understand your choices, and if you listen carefully, the practice will help guide you to better decisions.

Today, create your own mind time by setting aside fifteen minutes of time daily in which you are quiet with yourself. Allow no negative words or thoughts during this time, but answer the questions "Who am I?" and "What do I want in order to be healthy and productive?" and "What work do I need to engage in to make this happen?"

April 15

You were not random,

An act of unknowing,

A settling

For comfort.

No, you were

Intentional,

A choosing,

An act of selecting,

Not perfection

But partnership.

I choose to

Love all of you.

When you choose a life partner, you should do so intentionally. An intentional choice in a partner does not mean there are no problems along the way, but it does give you freedom.

In fact, you may have intentionally selected an adventurer though you are a homebody. All partnering comes with compromise. When you choose a partner, you make a commitment to compromise.

Today, choose your partner all over again with the power of intention. Know that there are differences and there will always be compromise. Let your partner know that you have decided again to share your life and heart as an intentional choice. See where the conversation goes.

April 16

Messages sent
Wrapped with
Protection.
Each color
Each ring
Gently
Surrounds a
Fragile package.
They will
Break your
Fall.
The message
Is strong
But you
Still must
Jump.

We all have people who support and guide our growth and learning. Those people are important to our journeys, but they cannot take the journeys for us. We must take our own small steps and eventually trust ourselves to jump.

We often stay stagnant, with our self-talk keeping us from the jump, afraid that we may fail or that the jump may cause change or pain. It may do both of those things, but we still have to make the choice to go.

Today, consider where you are stagnant and afraid of the next step in your journey. Talk with the person who supports you, and determine how you can move to the next place in your journey.

April 17

Chaos surrounds.

With angry fear

Projected

Onto my screen,

I view

From a position

Of choice.

Using wisdom and

Understanding choice,

I decide to jump in

Or move to a new screen.

Making decisions and life choices using your own wisdom is the best way to live a full and productive life. We find ourselves saying, "I know I need to …" or "You're right, but …" to other people. We need to examine whether we believe what we are saying and why we aren't acting on our own beliefs.

Understanding our choice includes knowing why we made the choice and how we determined that it was a good choice. This is the first step to wisdom-based decision making. Acting on what is right rather than what is easy is the next step. Wisdom-based decision making must begin and end every day.

Today, begin your wisdom decision making by examining a recent choice you made that is bothering you, and how you made the decision. Decide what is right to do, and start your change process today. Repeat each day deciding what is important to you, and when it doesn't go well, start anew the next day.

April 18

Take
A journey
To the very
Limit of
My inner being
And through
The vastness
Of the
Sea.
Come discover
Your art
Traveled inside
All levels
Because we
can.

Allowing positive and encouraging people to travel with you and to know you authentically is a gift. Only a few people will be allowed this kind of access to you, so make sure that the people you allow in are healthy to your spirit.

It is easy to close off your spirit to others after you have been hurt; you can guard yourself so carefully that no one is allowed in to know the real you. A lonely spirit isn't a healthy spirit. Balancing to ensure that you allow healthy people while guarding your spirit is positive.

Today, reflect on the people who know the authentic you and provide your spirit healthy encouragement. If your spirit is lonely, reach out to one you know encourages you and begin the process of letting her or him have access to you. If you feel like you have someone who knows you, give that person a call and thank her or him for being part of your positive spirit.

April 19

I set my frame,

My view on

How my heart

Perceives

My daily brushes

With

Juggling, jarring, and jolting,

A day's grind.

I determine

Even on those hard days

To experience

Joy.

Every day brings some struggle and some joy, but the joy can be buried beneath the daily grind and all the noise of the day. You have a choice in what you uncover each day.

Choosing joy with all of the difficulties and stresses we face every day can be a daunting task. When we choose joy at the end of the day, we will find happiness all around us.

Today, take a look around at the world around you and find the 100+ things that are small joys. They may include the beauty of a spider web or the simple sound of laughter; there are small joys all around us. Remember the things you find today on the days when you can't seems to find any joy.

April 20

Two masters—
One of duty, faith,
And promises,
One of passion
And learning.
Each tears
Pieces of my
Heart and soul
To find its
Place
Within me.
I wonder,
When they
Are done,
Will I
Be able to
Find me?

Having a family and a career provides two very different ways you fill your heart. Both family and career give and take in different ways. There are always choices that must be made.

If you have a career that is a passion, it is hard to turn it off to give the necessary care to your family. Understand that having it all does not happen. There are choices to be made.

If you continue trying to make everything work out equally, it tears at you and you can lose yourself. Today, examine your own tug-of-war with having it all. Verbally forgive yourself and provide the affirmation that your choices are accepted with peace. Continue to work at providing yourself the peace and grace of accepted decisions.

April 21

At my hand,

Tools of

Healing and hurt.

In control,

I choose

Which instrument

I provide

To one

In need.

Both make lasting

Imprints—

One a scar,

One a new landscape.

Always in control,

My choice is

Simple.

All people have in their power the ability to heal or hurt those connected to their lives. We often lash out at those we most care about and believe forgiveness is never-ending, but the scars we leave are permanent; even if they heal, they leave a lasting mark.

We can choose how we affect those around us. It is important that we take control of the tools we have within our reach to create positive and healthy environments for those who cross our paths daily.

Slow down today and begin to recognize your own positive tools—your words, deeds, and touches. Find two people you interact with daily, and use your positive tools to enhance their day.

April 22

You have touched
Me,
Wrapping yourself
Around me,
And I cannot
Seem to
Stop you.
Your power
Frightens me
Yet draws me to
You at the
Same time.
I wonder,
Which way will
I run?

Some people influence and affect us in strong and life-changing ways. Stop running from these people, as they have a way of catching you. Face those people who seem to have power over you, and understand that *you* provide the power to *them*.

You have the ability to determine who has access to you and who does not. To have the ability to choose, you first need to recognize your own power. Then, with quiet strength, no longer provide access to those people who frighten you or engage you in negative thinking.

Today, stop running, and be thoughtful about those people who push your buttons for a negative response. What might your day look like if you turned off those buttons? Begin the process of directing your power to only those who bring positive light.

April 23

I choose

Happy

Inside my mind, heart, and voice

Even when I am

Faced

With challenge

And struggle

Because I choose.

My actions

Must follow

With the truth

Of my

Happiness.

Although you cannot always choose your circumstances, you can choose how you react and what your attitude will be. You do control your response to the situations and circumstances that come your way. Your responses can send you into a positive direction or down a destructive path.

Eventually, you choose your mindset. A positive mindset will serve you and others with a better approach. You often have to work at a positive mindset, because it needs to filter through your mind, heart, and voice in order for your actions to follow.

Reflect on the choice of attitude that you have selected during a difficult situation. Examine whether you are choosing a positive reaction. Make a choice to be positive in your attitude.

April 24

Drifting
Forcefully with
Purpose,
You imprint
Yourself.
You are drifting
On my
Spirit.
I cling
To the
Rock,
Waiting, watching,
Wondering.
Will I set myself
A drift
Or
Silently watch
You drift
Away?

It is easy and almost unnoticeable to drift through life and allow others to drift into your life. When you choose to engage in drifting, one day, you suddenly realize you don't know how or when you got to this point in your life.

Whether that life point is weight gain or an unconnected relationship, you need to recognize that you chose it by allowing your life to coast by without using intention. When we become passive by waiting, watching, and wondering what other people may do, we are drifting.

Take action in the areas of your life that are just drifting, and create an action plan that engages you in choosing a new course.

April 25

The panic,

The anxiety swells

Inside

Your chest.

I want to

Calm, settle,

But

My panic

And anxiety

Swell until

They swallow

Me

Whole.

When panic and anxiety strike, it is difficult to recognize or implement our choices. This is the time to slow down and bring in healing breath that centers us by our choice.

We can get stuck in a very dormant place and find it difficult to move. The important step is recognizing that we are stagnant out of fear or anxiety. Then we can slowly and intentionally work our way beyond the barriers.

Today, take time to think about an area of your life that makes you anxious, and determine if the anxiety is keeping you from moving forward. Then think about completing a calming meditation, or visualization to help remove the feelings keeping you from moving forward. Keep at this until you are able to move forward.

April 26

Each choice
Affects
The person
You are becoming,
But there is change
In choice,
As a
Choice
Is one page
In a larger
Story.

We have all made choices that were not in our best interests or perhaps were risks that did not work the way we thought they might. Although such a choice affects our lives, we can make changes in our paths.

One of the best things about choice is that it allows you to make changes in your life. We can choose to alter course or even begin a new course. All of our choices are small parts of our larger story.

Today, examine a choice you made with the effects you wish to change. Be analytical in your examination, and determine what led you to the choice you made. Do you need to alter the path or do you need a new path? What steps will you need to take if you engage in a new choice? Don't be stuck; decide to engage in the choice process.

April 27

Risk
To trust
My heart,
My life,
To believe
In what
No one
Else
Can feel,
To give up
Control,
To risk.

Having the confidence to believe in choice will coexist with the willingness to risk. Although the risks can be balanced with wisdom, risks still have an element of the unknown. People who use choice as a tool are resilience. The feeling of being in control is often based on a false sense of security, and when we are in jeopardy, those feelings can lead to choices of safety. We don't have control over everything that comes our way, but we have choices to examine. Living a full and productive life will require you to take the unknown path, a risk, at times.

Believing in yourself is the first step in allowing yourself to take risks. Strengthen your resilience and learn the skills of risk-taking, and know that you can stand again if you fall. Allow your dreams to become reality by taking the unknown path.

April 28

Gazing at the
Universe of stars,
I am one small
Piece of a larger
Family.
My choices won't
Change the stars
But may
Change the way
Those close
To me view
Them.

It is so easy to say, "It doesn't matter," because sometimes we feel so insignificant that we think what we do and say don't make a difference in the universe. But every day, you make a difference to those in your family, so it *does* matter.

The choices you make have a direct impact on those you love. Even early decisions like your child not taking school seriously can impact his or her life.

Today, reflect on your own choices and how they have affected those you love. Take the words "it doesn't matter" out of your vocabulary and understand how much it does matter.

April 29

Bright oranges, fire-red
Urgent purples, yellows, and
Brilliant blinding streams of white
Are unleashed.
Within my cool blueness
Lives deep hot color.
I find myself
Exploring, teaching, experiencing
New shades of me.
Come share my colors.

There is someone important you need to choose to know: you. It is easy to stop knowing who you are when you meet everyone else's needs. Only you can decide to make yourself important.

When you are important to yourself, you choose to know what you like and how you want to grow and develop as a person. Knowing who you are is a priceless gift not just to yourself but also to those you love.

Have you decided to make yourself important? It may be the most vital decision you make. You have to put your own oxygen on before you help those you love.

April 30

Choice is freeing
And powerful
Choices provide
Hardship
Of ownership
But allow each
To smile
With knowledge
That this
Is
Me.

In this month of reflecting and acting on choice, it is important to remember how powerful that understanding choice is, as well as how powerful it is to accept the ramifications of our choices.

There is great freedom in owning our choices and also understanding that we can choose to make needed changes. When you make a change, you should expect a struggle, even embrace the struggle. We learn and we gain strength when we own what we do.

Think through the month and reflect on your current choices. Which of your choices make you balanced and happy? Which of your choices do you need to reframe into opportunities? Bring action to your choices throughout the year.

May

During the month of May, we take time to rejuvenate our internal life-force and the spirits of those who cross our paths daily. This month, take time to slow down enough to become aware of the status of your spirit.

As you take stock of your own internal force, make sure you are nourishing yourself before you provide to others. This will ensure that you are able to be a lifelong giver to others. In giving to others, reflect on whether you are trying to fix the problem or are providing the light and encouragement for others to work things out on their own.

Your inner space is powerful and can steer you in many directions. Take this month to center and balance the strength of your spirit to bring yourself peace of mind.

May Focuses

The spirit matters.
Nurturing yourself.
Nurturing others.

May 1

Whispering
Inside myself
The words
My spirit craves
Encouragement
Empowerment
Emotion
There is saturation
Filling my desert
Allowing me to grow
Others.

It is important to engage in daily positive conversations with yourself. You cannot consider yourself a positive person unless you are positive with yourself, including in the internal conversations you have.

The words and tones you use with yourself are important to empowering you as a person. If many people depend on you during the day, please know that your own mindset and spirit need your attention first.

Today, listen to your internal conversations. Begin to remove all words that do not encourage you, empower you, or fill you with positive emotion. Being truthful with yourself does not have to be a beating but can be done with kind words. Plan a positive conversation with yourself as the sun goes down, and determine when you can have regular positive conversations with yourself.

May 2

Even alone,

Someone connects

To me with a dinging

Message,

Continual chatter

Needing response,

Taking away

The calm solitude

Needed

To nurture

The internal

Spirit

I call

Me.

Connection with other people is essential to your well-being but must be balanced with individual and personal connection with yourself. Other people now have access to us on demand, 24/7.

The wonderful electronics that keep us in the know also keep us from nurturing our internal spirits. We can go days, even weeks, without having time to acknowledge who we are and to dream about who we want to be. The wires and continual chatter keep us from finding out that we have lost the ability to connect with the most important people— our internal selves.

Today, take one hour to disconnect from all of the technology to stop and listen internally. If you have trouble connecting to your internal voices, try disconnecting daily, until your voice stops talking about lists and other people and tells you about you.

May 3

Soul hungry
For loving words
And hands of care
To whisper
To those I
Serve.
It is
Me
Who
Reaps benefit
Of whispering
Care to
Others.

We gain much by serving others. You do not have to formally volunteer to gain daily. Serving others can include letting another car in to traffic or asking, "How are you?" to a coworker and listening to the response.

Serving others who need a connection to your smile betters your world. The best gift it provides is the way it fills your own spirit and creates a healthier you.

Today, find first a close family member to provide loving words or a helping hand to. Don't let the person know your assignment—just serve in a way you know will help. Second, whisper care to a coworker or a stranger. See if you want to repeat the work each day.

May 4

Partake in community elements,

Joined hearts,

By speaking and listening.

Bring internal and external worlds

Together.

Coexistence without interaction

Leaves

A lost heart.

The people you choose to spend time with are significant and may mean the difference between a lost heart and a joined heart. Your communities and those places you spend a great deal of time need to maximize your positive attitude and fill you with health.

Your selected communities are the people you spend the most time with each day. If TV characters are filling your time, you need to rethink your community, because interaction with others is what creates positive energy in your life.

Reflect on your communities and which you spend the most time with daily. Determine if the interactions are providing you positive energy. Make changes to increase the positive energy, and thank those in your communities today.

May 5

Inside anger
    Quietly shuts the petals,
Withdrawing one by one,
    Until
The flower, like a black beetle
    On a stem,
Tipping and teetering
    Until
The stem breaks
    And
The black beetle
    Is shattered
Into a thousand shiny pieces.

Allowing anger to shut down your spirit closes you off from the positive aspects of life and can eventually break you into pieces. Internal, hidden anger is the most destructive kind of anger, because it leads your heart and actions to places that are unproductive to you and those you love.

We all have anger and get angry. Anger is a normal part of living. It is when we hold the anger in tightly without release that we are in danger. Recognizing the anger is the first step. Acting to release it in a healthy way is the next step.

Today, fully examine your own peace of mind and heart. If you are holding on to anger, begin by having a conversation with yourself about what the anger is and what might release you from the feelings. Start with what you have to change before approaching another person to fix your anger. Then take three deep breathes and visualize releasing the anger.

May 6

Cleaning day
Gives the
Spirit
A day to
Celebrate
Ordinary
Pleasures
Of daily
Living.

Clean sheets and shined counters provide a lift to your spirit. We often view cleaning as drudgery, but it brings calm and a centering inside. Today, begin to view cleaning as a pleasure and something to celebrate.

Changing your view of the daily tasks you need to get done helps with procrastination and can bring a smile while you are doing those everyday tasks. Finding happiness in the ordinary can lift your mood.

Today, find a small task needing done, and before beginning, take a moment to celebrate the ordinary. Take pleasure in doing the task rather than just being glad it's done. See if the approach makes you smile.

May 7

Walls
Suffocate
Who you
Are.
They force you
To channel
Out
And leave
Your essence
In safety.
But they
Will not
Keep you
Safe,
Only bury
You
In unbreakable
Stillness.

We all put up walls, thinking they will protect us from hurt, but walls block out all that can heal us, including working through the hurt. Living fully involves breaking down walls and acting on forgiveness.

Only the act of forgiving both internally and externally will break you free of the walls you have so carefully put up. The walls block engagement in life. The freedom of forgiveness brings fresh air into a stagnant place in your heart, immediately bringing healing.

Today, determine where you have built a wall of protection, and forgive yourself for building and keeping it. Be determined to forgive the person or circumstances involved in the construction of your wall. In your daily thinking, keep forgiving.

May 8

Beautiful brown eyes filled
She is so sad
I want to empty her sad
She determined unable
To refill.

We all have loved ones and friends who struggle and for whom we want to make things better. Sometimes we begin to think we can just make it better for them. But we can't. Each person has to decide to allow a refilling of his or her internal spirit, and to be determined to do it. We can keep connected with them and hopeful that they are open to replenishing their hearts and spirits.

Allowing another to hold his or her own spirit is a struggle for those of us who want to nurture, but it is essential for an authentic spirit to emerge. Holding one's own spirit requires personal work that no one can do else can do.

Today, if you have a loved one who is struggling, release yourself from fixing his or her spirit, because you can't. Instead, reach out and continue to provide encouragement, letting the person know that she or he is empowered to fill her or his own spirit.

May 9

His spirit entered me
Without knowledge of his power.
What was thought as a passage
Created a lifelong yearning of
Controlling, focusing, and moving,
Allowing his spirit to stay buried.
Now with open heart,
His buried spirit is flowing
Through all that I am.

Many pass through your day and have an impact on you. The people who become part of your spirit should be honored for what they have helped you learn and for how they helped shape the current you. Sometimes these are people who are with you for your whole life, and sometimes they passed through but changed you forever.

Honoring those who have affected you is important to honoring your own spirit. It provides a connection to your past, present, and future. Don't be surprised if some of those people are those you have struggled with during your journey. If they helped you grow, honor that growth.

Today, think about those who have affected you. Find a way today to honor those people and have gratitude for the impact they have made. Write a thank-you card to those who allowed your potential to thrive.

May 10

Body, spirit, and mind
Earth-connected,
Providing the
Water, sun, and air
To those passing through
Our paths,
Regenerating
And connecting
Body, spirit, and mind.

The earth around you is a true rejuvenator when you truly connect to and become grounded in her awesome and powerful beauty. You don't need to be in a national park, because you can find a connection to the earth out any window. Becoming aware of the earth around you heals your spirit.

Taking daily time to feel the sun on your face or to watch the passing clouds is important to connecting to yourself and to others. Every season and every place has its own special presence to engage in every day.

Don't make your earth connection random. Make a time to give gratitude to the earth and soak in the power of the ground you call home. Make an effort to change one habit to ensure that you help the earth keep its balance.

May 11

Storms inside her.

She,

Steady, strong, and sturdy

Internally,

Rides her storm

Alone

But provides

A light

For others.

Riding storms alone is risky. Those not willing to ask for help or to include others during their internal storms will have the light they shine for others dim and then eventually go out. Strong people often struggle with including others in their difficulties, but this is a necessary skill to develop.

The stronger person will begin to recognize that holding it all together alone is not healthy. We are stronger when involving the right people in our circles. This strengthening will allow our lights to continue for others.

Today, think about the internal storms you are facing. Who are the people you choose to include in your struggle? These can be counselors, friends, a circle of people you know have your best interests at heart. Begin to include others to strengthen your light.

May 12

I will whisper

To his

Spirit

Each day

That

His actions and words

Are

Kind and gentle,

That

What he thinks

Matters.

I will nurture

His heart

So he believes

And whispers

To his son.

We all have a commitment to the next generation. Teaching kindness and compassion by our words and our actions is essential to making our world better. We need to be direct in our teaching.

It is important that we pass forward our wisdom and ensure that our children and grandchildren know that what they think and do matters. It is important that the next generation learns to whisper your knowledge.

Find a younger person to spend time with today, and be intentional in your whispering. Make sure your words are nurturing and help bring value to the day to day living. Tell the younger person that she or he needs to pass on what you are saying to the generation that will follow.

May 13

Surf's crashing waves

Tell me

Of ongoing

Need to live

Each moment

Riding the up

And down

Feeling

Salt, air,

Spirit spray.

Staying present requires us to be brave. Living in the past or wondering what the future will bring is easy because they aren't in front of you. The moment in front of you is living.

We face ups and downs daily, and how we react to those daily ups and downs may determine the choices we have in the future. Nothing changes yesterday, but the moment you are in can be lived fully.

Today, recognize the power of today and how you are riding the waves of just today. Take time to realize that you are living today, and make sure you take steps to make today count as a great day. It will fill your spirit.

May 14

My internal voice

Tells an open heart

Life's truths.

My heart

Hears the truth,

But listening,

I

Fear

The words

And actions

Needed to

Live fully in

Truth.

A healthy, vibrant living soul not only listens to its internal voice but is determined to act with word and deed in alignment. Your internal voice can guide you to bold actions that allow you to live fully.

One of the most freeing and joyous moments in life is when you give up trying to be what others want or allowing others to define you. It takes courage to risk being yourself and to have your actions reflect your own life's truths.

Today, take time to listen to your own internal voice and determine one or two actions that will help you live more authentically with your own internal voice.

May 15

Spirit drums
Pound
A beat into
Earth,
Who
Supports
My body
And allows
The drum force
Into
My small spirit
To beat
Old living
And new thinking
Into the world.

Connecting to your patch of earth and finding the beat that flows through the ground encourages a connected spirit. You don't have to travel to find the earth beating life into those taking its energy; you just have to take time to appreciate the beating flow given to you.

Those who take the time to find the earth's energy and gifts receive an awakening as well as an easing of pain. Finding the earth's energy requires time away from phones, computers, and, sometimes, other people, and requires only a small patch of the earth's forest, desert, marsh, or backyard.

Breathe in the sounds, smells, colors, and beating of something larger than yourself. Find a moment to be humble and recognize that the earth provides a new morning to you every day and allows you to think about your world in new ways.

May 16

Whale breathing
I stop
To only
Breathe.
A function,
A gift,
It fills
Lungs and heart,
And then in
My quiet,
My spirit gains
Needed
Life.

Breathing is essential to living, but it also is a tool for filling and comforting your spirit. Deep belly breathing filling every corner of your lungs and body, followed by a complete exhalation, brings needed relief.

This type of deep breathing can assist you in your quiet-spirit moments. Being aware of and working on your breathing is beneficial before you ground yourself to the earth or have your daily spirit conversation.

Practice deep soothing breathing several times today. Watch your belly fill, and then exhale while working to relax your shoulders, hips, and toes. Try this healing breathing before making connection to your spirit.

May 17

Celebrate and
Honor
Those
Spirit whisperers
Who
Encourage
Embolden
Empower
Those
Passing through
Their life
Classrooms.

It is important to take time to honor and celebrate those people who have been your spirit whisperers. There are several ways to honor those who take time to encourage, embolden, and empower others.

Taking the time to encourage, embolden, and empower others is one of the best ways to honor someone who gave you the gift of a lifted spirit. Spirit whisperers don't give to others to be noticed but provide the quiet nurturing needed to better someone's life.

Today, find one of your spirit whisperers and tell him or her about the impact that the whispering had on your life. Then honor this whisperer by giving a quiet whisper to someone in your life who needs a boost.

May 18

Finding strength

And value

In one

Building on

Those skills

And gifts

Provides

A mirror

To one

And tells

A story

Worthy of

Repeating.

Being a spirit whisperer requires looking for the gifts found in others. A spirit whisperer provides a mirror to others, allowing them to see their gifts.

When others are able to recognize that they are special and have skills, they grow. They have the opportunity to enhance what is already there. Once a person has encountered a spirit whisperer, she or he is likely to become a spirit whisperer to others.

Today, be a mirror for another person. Take time to show that person his or her gifts not by listing the gifts but by describing what you see the person doing and saying. You will get better at whispering the more you do it.

May 19

Encouraging myself

First

Is not

Selfish

But is needed

In order

To nourish

A new soul

In the seat

Next to

Mine.

We tend to think of encouragement as something we freely give to others, but encouragement starts with ourselves. It is important to encourage our dreams and ourselves when things aren't going well.

Although you may have others who encourage you, never wait for outside encouragement. Begin the encouragement with your words and actions aimed to give yourself a boost. Be intentional about the conversations you have with yourself to ensure that the words are empowering to you.

Today, begin providing yourself daily encouragement around a specific goal or dream. Listen to your reaction, and don't allow negative or passive responses. Remember that you must replenish yourself before giving to others.

May 20

Dirt between fingers

Dark rich

It smells of

Past, present, and future

It provides

A Peace

That allows my

Heart to focus

On only

The watermelon seed

Placed in safe

Warm dirt

To Grow.

Connecting to the earth and feeling the power of what the earth provides to us daily lifts our spirits. The earth nurtures us while we give back using small seeds. Although we are not all gardeners, we all need to give back to the earth.

Get your hands in the dirt, even if it's only in a small pot on your windowsill or a plot in your backyard or a community garden. Make your part of the earth better.

Start today. Buy a few seeds or plan what you will plant in your pots. Don't be discouraged by a brown thumb; keep trying to make your part of the earth green.

May 21

Immediate shift

With an external

Stretch

The lines

On my face

Move up

Shoulders relax

Toes wiggle

And I smile

To myself

Again.

Smiling is simple, easy, and powerful. Every time you smile, you release rejuvenating chemicals into your body that help you cope with the many stresses you encounter daily. Smiling to others with your face and eyes creates human connection.

It also releases powerful chemicals throughout the other person's body, ensuring that she or he can better cope with the world. Sometimes, summoning the effort to give a smile to someone provides just the connection that the other person needed.

Today, practice smiling to yourself. Feel your body's reaction to smiling, and notice if you feel like you have more energy. Throughout the day, also smile at those you come in contact with, and reflect on your impact on them.

May 22

Grant yourself

Permission to discover

Your passions,

Those lights

And sparks

That charge

You and renew

Your energy

And set your mind

To make

The world alive

And better

Because

You had passion.

Give yourself permission and blessing to discover and invest in your passions. Living with your passion is a gift, and when you are alive with passion, your spirit is filled with energy.

Our passions are about our interests and what makes us better people when we invest time and energy into them. They only need to make us happy and to engage our spirits in positive energy.

Today, do one thing that engages your interests and your passion. Make sure you give yourself permission to engage. Don't wait for another day to pass, because passionate people make the world better.

May 23

Open
Breathing and balancing
Teaches
Me daily
To release
My heart
To new
Opportunity
And allow
My internal being
To learn.

Breathing is not only essential to living but can provide the needed ingredients to a healthy spirit. Practicing full breathing from your belly daily releases pressure and stress.

When we release with breathing and balance, we begin to open up to the opportunities around us every day. Through breathing, we free our internal selves to learn.

Take today to practice deep breathing and centering. It is important to breathe in fully and release fully. Feel the breath enter and exit. Send out the stress and blockers, and breathe in opportunity.

May 24

Gathering family,
Generations mixing
In conversation—
Fathers, mothers, children
Creating connections
To my soul
And life's future.

Bringing the generations of your family together to engage in conversation boosts everyone's feeling of connection. Connecting across generations builds understanding of our common ground and forms compassion around our differences.

When it is possible, include children at the table so they are part of the conversation rather than isolated at their own table. Disconnect them from their electronics, as it is important that they learn how to have conversation and are exposed to new ideas.

Plan an event in which your family (whoever you define as a positive group of people) is together. Be intentional about integrating the generations. It doesn't have to be an elaborate dinner, just time together to hear stories and talk about meaningful issues. The connection will keep your spirit soaring.

May 25

Holy passion,

A profound mystery

Transcends and transforms

Through

Joy.

Sacred fires burn within.

To leave

These fires untended

Is to feel your

Soul decompose

In life.

Your life's passion is the path to transforming an ordinary life to a life of authentic joy. We often think we will tend to our passions when there is time or when we retire, but today is the moment to spend with your passion.

To leave your passions untended is to experience a slow death while living. It is important to nurture your passions even if you need to engage with them using small steps.

Today, nurture your spirit by enjoying one of your passions. Develop a plan to give yourself time for something you love. Continue to tend to your passion now rather than waiting for the right time to come.

May 26

Filling spaces and time

Busy

Ensuring no moments to

Feel

I make sure the

Intense

Emotions I carry

Hide

So none

Surface

And make me

Face

The hurt.

It is easier sometimes to fill our lives with one task after another to keep busy. It allows us to survive the hurt we don't want to deal with or face. Work can be a powerful healer if it is not used to mask our feelings and if we balance it with internal work.

Believing that you don't have time for internal thinking may be a sign that you are just surviving. Internal nurturing brings new creativity and energy to your external work. Those things that you feel intensely and are afraid to let surface block you from experiencing a full life.

Decide to live a fully balanced life by engaging with your internal self and working to nurture your spirit. If you are struggling with deep hurt, begin today by telling a friend, and then consider finding a counselor to work with you.

May 27

Present in my spirit

Each day

An inward turn

For scrubbing

And reshaping

Alignment

To my core

Value of

Living.

To maintain a healthy spirit, you need to be fully present with your spirit each day. Making sure to check in with your internal self to align and sometimes realign to your value system is part of nurturing your spirit.

The inward check is a daily period when you have time for quiet reflection and conversation with yourself. There is always time for things you believe are important. The important things can be incorporated into a daily drive with no radio or phone interruptions, but you must make time every day for them.

Today, make an appointment with your spirit. During your appointment, take stock of how positive or negative you are feeling, and make adjustments so the positive wins the day.

May 28

There is a calling

Meeting your

Value and purpose.

It awakens

Both fear and courage.

Answer your calling

To begin your

Real work

And gain

Contentment.

Each person has a special calling in this life. It isn't always a job but a passion that brings out happiness and great contentment in the person. We often drift through life and make our calling wait.

You can start meeting your value and purpose by first starting to recognize your calling and then taking steps to realize your important work. Beginning to realize your passion can be as small as starting the garden you have always wanted in small patio pots, or making the jump to change your career.

Today, list your passions and pick one that stands out; this is a calling. Take two steps to start making your calling a reality. Tell one close person your dream.

May 29

See the beauty lining your path.

Be amazed at the flower growing

Between the rocks.

Hear the breeze rush past your face.

Allow yourself to listen to the smallest rustle

Of grass bending.

Touch the rain falling off the roof,

Drinking in the coolness in your palm.

Know the miracle of the cloud burst.

Sense your own happiness.

With eyes open,

Breathe in your own

Joy.

Each day brings an opportunity to find beauty in your surroundings. When you find beauty, your soul finds peace and a special kind of joy. Look for and find the beauty in unusual places, like the saguaro giving homes to your neighborhood birds.

Joy is within your grasp; you can create it with just your surroundings. You need to be able to sense happiness in your own backyard. Those little miracles are the ones that bring you happiness.

Today, use your senses to fill your soul with joy and happiness. Find one or two miracles in your own backyard.

Smile and find peace of mind.

May 30

Over thinking,

Ensuring sequential

Logic,

Masking

The most beautiful things

That are not seen or touched

But felt

Through a heart

Touching

The inner self.

Our logic and sequential thinking are important, but if not balanced with feeling and emotion, they can block us from sensing the things in this world that are not physically here but are here, just the same. Using only one set of thinking will cause you to miss half of the world.

Opening your feelings and emotions is scary. When you compete in a world that often ignores or discounts emotions, it is easy to turn off your emotional side, but this side offers a great deal to you and to your world.

Think about an area of your life that you continually think about and use logic in while you solve problems. Today, use your feelings to solve problems in that area. Start with the simple words "I feel …" and see where that takes you. Don't discount those feeling statements.

May 31

Giving unlocks
Life's fullness and
Awakens an internal
Spirit,
Turning our worldly
Good into plenty.
Nurturing breaks
Chaos to order and
Confusion to clarity,
Yielding a teacher and
A learner.
Connecting brings
Internal peace
And quiet breathing,
Creating a spirit
Of joy.

For your internal spirit to flourish and thrive, you must nurture, give to, and connect to others and yourself regularly. Your sense of self and your spirit are important to a healthy, centered, and balanced life.

When your internal view of the world is grounded, you are able to meet your potential and become both teacher and learner—one who gives and who is able to take from others with gratitude.

Connecting with others and self allows us to find joy and contentment in the ordinary and routine while being pushed to be active dreamers. You built your internal being this month, but remember it is important to be active in the things you learn. Take three ideas that struck you from this month's conversation and actively pursue them as part of your daily life.

June

Every stage of life is a celebration. It is important to enjoy the journey and to make sure that you recognize that continual growth occurs throughout your life. You provide the attitude, actions, and aptitude to always be learning about yourself and your world.

Growing throughout your life is powerful to keeping young in heart and spirit. Perpetual growth requires that you do what you can to keep your body healthy but also to keep your mind and spirit healthy. Being mindful of your own self-talk and keeping yourself open to possibilities is essential.

Aging is a gift that we often overlook. Aging is not about getting old but about growing into new opportunities at each stage of life. Aging is honoring where we are presently as well as honoring where we have been, but aging is also about being ready for the future.

June Focuses

Growing is powerful.

There is joy in the journey.

Every stage produces possibility.

June 1

Joyous middle of life
  Provides peaceful confidence.
No need to fill with words.
  I am
All the mistakes and learnings,
  Grayed, but shining
With secrets of middle life.

Something very special happens when you approach middle life. A quiet confidence comes about not because you have the answers but because you understand that the questions are much more valuable.

Middle age—whatever age it might be—accepts the mistakes that we have made as a part of what makes us who we are now. We may be graying, but we have the ability to shine inside for ourselves and others.

On this first day of June, whatever your age, take time to understand your mistakes as lessons. Determine what your important questions are, but don't ponder the answers; instead, make sure you are asking the right questions.

June 2

She knows her life plan,
    Details of future in place,
A story mirroring the fairy tale.

She questions what is left of her
    Schedules, needs of others
Whose story she is living.

She understands the questions,
    Works, building capacity and
Her own story.

She is in journey,
    Finds wonder in the steps,
    Time, experience, sharing,
And loving just who she is.

We all go through stages in life in which we think we know what the plans for our life are and stages in which where we question whose plan we are living. We are in continual change.

Even when we understand the right questions to develop our own lives, we are on a journey that should be enjoyed. Every stage is to be celebrated for what it brings to your character.

No stage is better than another, as they all have value. The journey is the important focus, and there should be wonder in each of your steps. Take today to stop and reflect on your current journey. How are you finding joy in your steps, and how are you sharing your journey with others?

June 3

The little girl,

The young woman,

The middle-aged mind—

She has always

Been afraid

Of the suffocating

Blackness,

Moved away,

Seeking light.

Now totally encompassed,

She gropes, feels, touches,

Finding finally the light

Inside

Herself.

Being afraid is a part of life. Finding your way through your fears is part of the wisdom that comes with age. The answers are not outside of us but inside our thoughts and feelings.

For many, growing up is a journey of finding your way through the fear, a journey we take on our own by feeling our way through the issue. Logic doesn't always find the light we are seeking.

Think about your fears. Sometimes we are afraid of doing the things that will create success in our life. Allow yourself to think about what is holding you back and how you can seek the light already inside you to overcome your fear. Age wisdom can guide you.

June 4

With intention

I seek

Friends with

The bravery to change

The status quo

Through their

Journey of accomplishment,

Ones who teach me

And teach with me—

Those facing aging

With the courage

To live.

Part of fully living in courage is being intentional in choosing the people you spend time with regularly. When you are surrounded with people making a difference, age doesn't matter.

People who can teach us new ideas and challenge us to change the status quo for better are worthy of inclusion in our journeys. Positive energy builds positive energy.

Time is our most precious resource, so we must utilize it to maximize our potential. Think about how you are spending your time and who you are including in your journey. Limit your time with those who drain you, and increase your time with those who live with courage.

June 5

Wait for the white horse

I am free and running

At my own

Pace,

Finding my own trails.

The white horse

Will need to

Be worthy

Of running with

Me,

For if he desires

To save

Me,

He will find me

Gone.

One of the best parts of growing to wisdom is being free of waiting for anyone to save me. With wisdom gained from years of learning, I know I am the person to save me.

Those wishing to capture or control you have no power to change you. Those wishing to run must keep pace with you, because there is great power in knowing that you can save yourself. This doesn't mean you don't need others but that you have the power to meet your own happiness needs.

Today, reflect on your ability to meet your own happiness needs, and if you are hoping for someone else to save you, ask yourself why. Begin to assess what makes you happy, and develop a plan to fulfill your happiness.

June 6

My thoughts

Maintain a fountain of youth,

Flowing new ideas,

Using creativity,

And bringing

Energy

To those I love.

Tapping water flow,

I defeat the

Definitions

Of those

Afraid of age.

Our thoughts are key to staying energetic while embracing where we are in life. Using new ideas and being involved in creating allows us to define ourselves rather than letting numbers define us.

Creating takes all kinds of forms, including a dinner that gives you pleasure, or rethinking how your living room is put together. Taking up a new craft or hobby can help energize you and cause new ideas and thinking to flow through you.

Today, focus your thoughts on new ideas in your life. Take direct steps to engage in using your creativity, and begin to define yourself by your thoughts and creativity rather than by a number.

June 7

Fragile now but
Managed almost a century
Of living
With rough hands
And eyes blurred,
With decades of pictures.
Strength runs
Through a curved spine,
And there is
Beauty
In small steps.

The journey of aging is not for the weak but for those with courage to face many physical, emotional, and cognitive changes. There is great beauty in the history and wisdom of those with steps that have become smaller.

Decades of pictures provide needed stories for the upcoming generations of learners. It is important that we make a connection to each generation, but we especially need to honor our oldest generation.

Today, plan an intergenerational event with your family. Connecting everyone around the table and ensuring that everyone has time to provide a story about what is important to them may be a great way to start. If that is not possible, get out to an elderly friend or a home for the elderly to make a connection. You will learn of the strength and beauty in those who have lived full lives.

June 8

There is a secret

I am holding.

It is hidden

In the folds

Of my face,

But it instills

A smile,

Creating one more

Wrinkle.

I am still the

Little girl, young woman

With those same

Feelings and thoughts.

Just the wrinkle has

Changed.

No matter what your age, you bring with you a life's worth of dreams. Some of the dreams no longer hold your interest, but you are still that person who had those dreams, and the vision and goals you had for yourself are still inside of you.

Those things that brought you special joy are important. Do not let a wrinkle or two stop you from achieving your dreams as long as they bring you happiness and keep you productive.

Today, think about those ideas you had as a young girl or as a young women. What did you forget about when life got in the way? What might bring you joy today? Make a list of what you want to keep in your life, and start working on the list.

June 9

Filled with opportunity,
Finding the courage
To begin a new stage
Of life.
A new stage is not lost youth
But a renewed
Chance to live
New possibilities
With
Wisdom.

Each stage of life provides a new set of opportunities. The benefit of having several stages behind you is that you are able to use past experiences and learning to dive into a new stage of life.

Your past experiences, even mistakes, are not a detriment but a tremendous benefit to your ability to be successful in new situations. It is important to be open to the new options that come your way and to view them using the wisdom gained from your past.

Gather up your courage to begin a new stage and determine a new challenge you are willing to try. Take one step to making that challenge one of your experiences.

June 10

Hopeful

seeking new thoughts

Giving

kindness and compassion freely

Choosing

happiness as a state of being

Having

gratitude with reverent truth

Secrets of an unwrinkled spirit

And heart of youth.

Many things keep us young at heart. We need to practice throughout life the things that help us and those around us to be better people.

Being hopeful in seeking new answers and freely giving kindness and compassion are a start at keeping your heart open. When you choose to be happy daily, you are discovering the most important secret to lifelong freshness. Along with choosing to be happy, working to be grateful for what you have will make your spirit resilient.

Today, be determined to practice the well-known secrets of an unwrinkled spirit; take time to look at a problem in a new way. Go out of your way to provide kindness to a person you love. Today, no matter what your circumstances, choose to be happy, and be grateful with deliberate thanks for what you have.

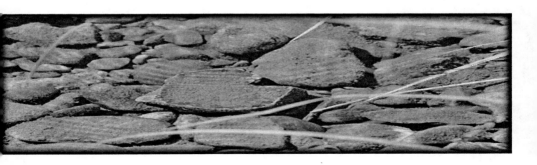

June 11

Although my shell

Is aged and carries

A sickness,

I am not

A victim.

This is part

Of the aging

Scenery,

But not what I

Engage inside my

Spirit,

As my spirit

Is immune

To changes in form

And understands a

Picture

Of healthy heart.

We all face changing canvases as we age. As our bodies age, the changes can weigh on our spirits unless we keep our spirits healthy. Engaging our spirits in productive and healthy habits will go far in the management of our bodies.

Positive thinking and actions keep our internal lights going, allowing us to keep ourselves getting up and finding purpose every day.

Take stock today of how you are reacting to your changing body. Are you instilling a positive feeling in your daily reflections? Provide yourself with two affirmations today that help you frame your thinking in a healthy way. Post them in a place you will see them every day.

June 12

In this time of my life,

Come play

Where I no longer

Fear dancing in the rain.

Come sing

Without a tune

To the songs

Of our youth,

For this moment is

The best time

For joy and raindrops

In this time of my life.

Many of us find it difficult to play because we have forgotten how to let go and be in the moment. We should play at every stage of life and teach our children that there is room in life for play.

Play comes in many forms. You alone may define what play is for you, but play should make you feel happy and should perhaps not be about crossing something off a list.

Each day offers moments open to play, even if only for a short time. Today, create a list of things that you consider play, and do one of them.

June 13

No turning back

Or looking again to see

What if

I look forward

To the possibilities

I encounter

With homegrown wisdom

And a knowledge bank

To shape my future

With

Resilience.

Resilience is a skill necessary for growing up and for staying engaged in a vigorous life. Being resilient requires leaving the past behind you.

There is no reason to ask "what if" when you are looking forward. The years of experience have provided you with the knowledge to shape your future.

Today, let go of whatever you have been second-guessing, and work to shape the future you desire. Pick yourself up and move forward. Let go with purpose and a conversation that allows you to move forward.

June 14

Told "don't cry,"
But years have
Taught me
Tears wash clean
The messes of the day
And the stresses of the
Heart.
Don't cry,
But my body
Yearns for the release
In the streams down my
Cheeks.
Cry.
The wise woman
Allows and accepts
Her tears
For the cleansing of
Mind, body, and spirit.

Crying is good for your soul. It is not a shameful act but a cleansing that is needed from time to time. The older I get, the less I fear what people might think about seeing me cry.

There are times we cry for good reason and times we cry for no reason. Either way, feel free to cry. Any kind of crying is acceptable: wailing, sobbing, or even just silent streams.

Today, accept your tears as healthy. You don't have to cry. You only need to give permission to yourself to cry when you feel like it. Don't be embarrassed by your tears, for they are cleaning your heart.

June 15

The leaf
Floats down.
Having given it
All to the host
I watch the leaf's
Wrinkled, dried
Form, so beautiful,
Fluttering to the
Ground,
A replacement
Needing space.
The leaf chooses
To fall
And provide
Enrichment to
The earth.

Many purposes call each of us to this life. It is important to answer your calling and to have no regrets when your time comes to move forward to the next purpose waiting for you.

Each stage in life provides a different purpose for you, whether raising a family or establishing a career. There is always another purpose waiting. We need to be ready for each purpose.

Today, determine what your next purpose might be, and think about how you are preparing for the next call. When one calling starts, another must end; how might you bring closure to your current work?

June 16

I am not in winter

For I am warm and alive

I do not wish for spring

When knowledge is new

Or summer

When living is filled with

Chaos

No, I am in autumn

The time of

Harvesting the good

We have sown

Through life

Allowing a giving back

To me

With a bounty

For others.

We often can feel we are in the wrong stage or perhaps that the stage doesn't fit where we are inside. You choose where you are and what you will take from the stage you are in today.

Even winter provides insight to life's problems, as does every moment you are living. When you have decided where you are in life, examine the stage for learning and what you will be able to give back to others after completing this time in your life.

Today, do not be afraid of where you are in life. Look deeply at what abundance is there and what you can give back to others. Then go outside of yourself and give.

June 17

I say with joy

I am 55

My age is a

Pleasure

A new stage

And I

Discover new ways

To think

With the courage

To act

On those 55-year-old

Thoughts

It is joy.

Being happy with your current age is hard for many, but knowing that each year allows another opportunity to make a difference in the world is a priceless birthday gift. It is important to push yourself to discover new ideas and to put into action your thinking.

Reframe your own thinking about what you lose with each year to what you gain and what you can give. When you begin each new stage of life with dread, you block new opportunities from opening to you.

Begin reframing your thinking today. Find one new way to engage your thinking and one activity that you have been afraid to tackle. Go for it and find the gifts given to you this year.

June 18

I am playing today

So I do not

Grow unable

To find pleasure

In indulgence

With a day

Of puddle jumping

And watching otters

At the zoo

I am playing

To grow my heart

Young.

Every day is a precious time—time to get things done and to cross off things on the to-do list. Because time is precious, it is very important to indulge yourself with play.

A life without pleasure is a life without happiness. Sometimes we get so busy that we let work be the only pleasure we have. To grow your heart, you need to give time to what you find fun and allow that fun to impact all areas of your life.

On this day in June, reflect on the last time you indulged yourself in a day (not an hour) of fun. Plan your next day to be fun, and don't let your excuses come into play. Indulge.

June 19

Learning to respect
Each generation
Young and old
Keeps alive in me
A creativity
Of thinking
That allows old
And new
To mesh into
A medium
I not only
Understand
But embrace
And respect.

Respecting the views and ideas of each generation allows for continued learning and growth. Each generation has its own individuality and unique experiences. We miss a great opportunity when we don't tap into this resource.

Grandparents, parents, children, and grandchildren can all learn from each other. It takes only one to model opening the dialogue and the door for understanding.

Today, be the model for opening the doors of understanding among the generations in your workplace, home, and any other place where you find multiple generations. Continue to learn from those older than you and those younger than you, and thank those teachers.

June 20

Redefining every age
Of life
Through the constant
Quest for learning
So aging
Is also
Redefined
Each year
And I find myself
Not growing old
But growing as a person
And defining
Who I am.

Some people define themselves as old or young, but defining yourself as a growing person may be healthier. Being able to redefine every age will require you to make changes in yourself through growth.

Making changes in yourself through learning will ensure that you are living out in the world and are engaged. Being a growing person means having conversation and activity with thriving people with meaningful interests.

Start today to redefine yourself as a growing person; no longer define yourself as old or young. Begin by finding those people who engage you in growing conversations. Find at least two new activities that will help you grow.

June 21

The surprise gift
Fills my day
With excitement
I am sure
Santa is real
My enthusiasm
Centers my days
And I will never
Outgrow
The capacity
To bubble
At the ordinary
For it keeps
Me smiling
And my heart
Ready to live.

Maintaining the ability to be excited by everyday life is part of growing your spirit. Excitement for life is not only great for yourself but is easily spread to others.

Decide to find things that you are enthusiastic about in your day-to-day life. It may not be wide-eyed "oh boy!" excitement, but allow your heart to feel it. That excitement may be about completing a project or changing something simple in your bedroom.

Today, decide that excitement is important to you, and make a commitment to find one thing you can be excited about each day. Spread the feeling.

June 22

Happiness does not
Appear in your life.
It requires building
Internal capacity
To be happy,
Increasing
Lifetime happiness,
Demands focus
And commitment,
So don't expect
Your later years
To be happy
If you have not
Built your own
Ability to be
Happy.

Being happy is a choice that you commit to work at each day. We tend to think of happiness as something achieved when we reach goals or when we get that one thing we have been wanting. When those things are over or don't last, are we left unhappy?

Happiness is not a state of being; it is a constant work to better ourselves and our world. You create your ability and capacity to be happy by those activities that engage you in productive, authentic improvement of yourself and your surroundings.

Today, decide that you are going to be happy, and then pick one small activity that makes you better and do one thing to make your community better. Take time to meditate on being better every day, and then work toward being better.

June 23

Now, in this
Moment, I
Live fully,
Not waiting for
Life to begin
Another day,
For scheduling life
To begin
Next week, next month, next year,
Or after this task
Leaves a
Wasted moment.

Waiting to begin living the way you want wastes precious time. Making time to live in the moment and to pursue those activities that make you a better person is a life beginning.

Although we all have schedules and time demands on us, we cannot put off those activities that help us pursue the things that bring joy to our lives—not momentary happiness but internal joy.

Begin today by not putting off that one activity that you have been waiting to do. Begin the planning, and work to complete the activity. Just make sure it is an activity that makes you a better person.

June 24

Every year marker

Enjoyed

Each with distinct merit

And growth

Adding wear on my face

And laugh lines

Like tree-trunk

Rings

Showing my personal

Life with drought and abundance

Grateful for

An added

Ring

And one more

Laugh line.

Be grateful for not only every day but every year. Although years will cause wear and tear, the truth is, each year is a blessing.

Don't be afraid of the years; be afraid of wasting them. Begin to take stock of how you are enjoying and celebrating your yearly markers. This doesn't mean big parties but productive reflection and gaining a sense of accomplishment.

Today, reflect on your own life rings and give thanks for your own years of drought and abundance. Plan how you might celebrate the experiences that provided you your beautiful laugh lines.

June 25

Simple growing
And learning
Ensure that you
Never repeat
Twenty-four again.
Getting older
Is not slowing down;
It is producing
A life with impact,
Without repeating
Youthful mistakes.

Ensuring that you don't repeat mistakes or relive the events of another year requires learning. It is important that you not only reflect on what you need to change but also to take on a new skill or hobby to create a learning environment for yourself.

Each year added needs a thoughtful examination of what new idea you will tackle—not the jump-out-of-the-plane one-time adventures, though they are also challenges, but the challenges that are long-term learning experiences. Think about something that will make you solve problems, create, or study.

Your additional skill set does not have to be developed at a birthday. If you haven't engaged yourself in building a new skill or new set of ideas, select something today.

June 26

I am not deprived

Of my age

Made

With every

Mistake

And success.

My road

Has been

An uphill and downhill

Journey.

No, I am my age,

Every moment

Earned.

You earn your age with the life you have lived. Mistakes and successes are what make us who we are and affect who we will be. It is important to celebrate every age we have earned and the privilege of moving forward.

Being happy with your age celebrates the journey that got you to today. Even the mistakes have been for the positive, as you have learned and become better because of them.

Today, do not deprive yourself of your age. Be proud of how many years you have experienced. Find a person who is younger than you, and shine the light on the positives of celebrating your journey.

June 27

Her mirror
Swirled with blue.
A prom dress.
And with a turn.
Her short white veil
Flicked in the mirror.
With a quick blink.
A frazzled Brownie leader
With hair pulled out of the way
The mirror—
A friend and foe.
She still turns
With a swish
Of peppered hair
And spots on her hands.
Her reflection
Is made of all
Days gone by,
But straightening
Her blue dress,
She looks forward.

In what seems a moment, a young girl moves to being a woman with gray in her hair and spots on her hands. Every stage is important and filled with growth and learning.

Honoring every stage of life and enjoying the journey brings contentment in your next phase. Moving through your days in survival mode can make it is easy to slip into survival as a way of life, but survival doesn't grow contentment with your life. Living in survival mode can grow anger and a feeling of waste.

Break out of any survival living you are doing, and honor your current passage by doing something you love doing by yourself. Smile and tell yourself ten things you like about being in this part of your life.

June 28

My children

Teach me daily

I am never too

Old to

Learn

About myself

And the

Ever-embarrassing

Things I have done

And said

By watching them

Repeat

Each embarrassment with

Proficiency.

Looking at yourself is best done through your children's eyes. Just make sure you bring your humor. Children have a perfect view and memory of every embarrassing moment you have ever had.

Being able to laugh at those moments is a key to a young spirit. Sharing those moments is even better because it not only brings laughter to others but also teaches them to take lightly those moments.

Today, share laughter with another person. Allow yourself to laugh at yourself and at those moments that make you cringe. It may help to know that your children will eventually have similar moments.

June 29

I plan to surprise you
Because I refuse to
Settle into predictability
I will walk in the rain
And order a beer
I will take the day off
And learn to paint
I will surprise you
And will
Work to surprise
Me.

Staying young in heart and soul requires us to venture outside of the daily rut we sometimes live in. Being able to surprise others is awesome, but being able to surprise yourself is even better.

Being open to new experiences and setting those experiences up for yourself is a huge part of keeping life full of surprise. Planning and scheduling all of our moments can stifle the surprises waiting for us.

Today, do something that might surprise your family, and then engage in something you haven't planned. Sense the excitement of surprise and enjoy the moment.

June 30

Growing wiser

Gives appreciation

And opportunity to

Be free,

Adapt, improvise, overcome

Stagnant, stale

Habits of mind and body;

Living with hope;

Creating ways to engage,

New states of living.

Reframe, reimage, reflect

A new self

With each year.

This month, we celebrated the wisdom gained in each stage of life. We alone are allowed to define what the current stage of life we are in means to us.

It is important to live each moment fully and with the freedom to overcome stagnancy in our lives. When we get preoccupied with aging and an assigned number, we lose, and we miss out on life.

Be willing to live each day with the option of new thinking. Allow yourself to redefine your habits and hopes continually. Take time to reflect on how you are living with age.

July

People study leadership and leaders. Leadership can be made into a very complex skill, and some people think one is a leader only when given a title, but we all have the opportunity to lead in our everyday lives and to influence others through the way we live.

Leadership has many sides and levels, and leading is difficult to do daily, as it requires us to do the right thing, to inspire others to take hard roads with us, and, perhaps most important, to carry the journey forward to improve our communities and other individuals.

We lead in our families, in our communities, and at work. Reflect this month not only on how you are leading at work but also on how you lead in your daily living. Most of all, know that you are leading, so be careful where you take people.

July Focuses

Leadership is not a position.

Leading is teaching.

Leading happens in everyday life.

July 1

Leadership is not

A job

A title

An authority.

It is a choice

To better those

You live with

Those you

Work with

Those you

Worship with.

It is a commitment

To make this world

And the people

You touch

Better.

We all have the opportunity to lead in our families, work, and communities. We don't need others to declare us leaders but need to choose to take on the tasks involved in making our world better.

Leading involves a commitment to model for others the behaviors that make your part of the world a better place to live and work. With the commitment will come the skills needed to lead people.

Today, make a commitment to be part of the leadership in the places that are important to you. Think about what you want to make better, and determine what your first step might be to make it better. Commit to taking that step.

July 2

You will be replaced

And jobs shifted,

But legacy leadership

Stirs encouragement

In others

To make better

Themselves and surroundings.

Embedded

And never

Replaced,

It allows improvement

To move forward.

Legacy leadership is not about leaving your name on a plaque but about ensuring that those you leave are able to continue important work and, most important, are inspired to make your work better.

This kind of leadership will require a new way of thinking as you encourage those around you to improve not only their surroundings but also their lives. Legacy leadership is needed in families, in friendship circles, in churches, and at work.

You have an opportunity to leave the people you love and the people you work with the inspiration to continue to get better. You can give no better gift to yourself and others.

July 3

There is no list
Defining perfect
Leadership,
As leading is
Personal,
Stemming from
Authentic honesty
And individuality,
Allowing others to
Truly
Believe.

There are books providing lists of characteristics of leaders. You will find some repeating characteristics, but not, perhaps, the most important. Leading is personal.

Leaders lead because what they are doing deeply matters to them. They have an authentic honesty about the work they are involved in trying to lead. This inspires others to believe in the cause.

Reflect on your own leadership characteristics. What truly matters to you in your day-to-day living? This is what is worth leading. You might find that what matters most to you is not your work but something else. Your individual traits are additional gifts that you bring to your leadership. Caring about leading the things that have meaning for you is a key to extraordinary leadership.

July 4

The easy road
Is an easy lead
But the hard road
Filled with possible
Stumbles and failures
Is often the right
Road.
Leading
The right
Road
Takes courage—
Not the chosen
Road for many
But the road
Where they should
Be.

Everyone has the opportunity to lead. Family, friends, and coworkers all provide leadership opportunities. When things are going well, the leadership road is easy. When you know in your heart that a different road is the right one is when leading becomes hard.

It is not an easy task to help people believe that the harder journey is the right one. It is even harder to take people them down a road that you as the leader know will contain some failure before the success.

The right roads require courageous leaders. Today, look at those you are living and working with each day. Are they on the right road or just an easy one? Visualize where you should be, and share that vision with one other person. Make plans for taking the right road.

July 5

Serving with true

Humility

Demands

That we teach others

To lead beyond

Our current limits,

Abandoning

Our own praise

To instill

In others

The ability

To serve.

Serving others is a gift. Teaching others to move beyond what we have is not only a gift but ensures that what we have worked to put in place continues and improves.

This means that things will be changed and adapted as they are continued. Serving with teaching not only helps others learn but also provides a model of serving without a need to hear our own praise.

When you serve, you are leading. When you serve and teach, you lead beyond your own limits and leave others to continue. Determine where you are currently serving, and decide what one skill you might teach to one other person this week in order to continue your vision of what is important.

July 6

Born with

One leadership instinct,

A backbone,

A leader

Must often stand

Strong but flexible

But while standing

Develop

A funny bone

And a wishbone

To support

The strong stand

Of the backbone.

All leaders require a backbone to make difficult decisions and stay the course during the hard times, but leaders must also develop humor and the ability to dream.

A leader who cannot laugh and help others laugh loses the chance to connect with others, as laughter is one of the most personal connections between people. Leading without the ability to dream is leading without the ability to improve the current situation. Leaders with backbone who dream their world better make it so.

Today, think about all three of your important leadership bones: your backbone, funny bone, and wishbone. Which do you need to strengthen? Determine steps to improve the one you most need to improve for your leadership.

July 7

There is purpose

In this moment

I am here

For a reason

In part,

My purpose

Is to throw

Bits of light

To lead

Others

Through

The dark

And into

Their own light.

Every person has a purpose to fulfill at this moment. We lead every day of our lives, at stop signs and in the grocery line. If part of our purpose can be to light the way for another person, that is wonderful. If, while providing light to someone struggling, we help that person find his or her own light, we have accomplished a great deal.

It is important to remember that we will not always be there to provide light and that helping others find their own light empowers them and creates light for the community.

The best way to allow people to find their light is to first listen to them with care and then provide guiding words of encouragement as they struggle to their own light. Today, light the way for someone and then listen for a way to encourage that person's light journey.

July 8

An authority
Determines to steer
Conversation
Her way
By the right of
Her title.
At the table,
An influencer
Makes an impact
With quiet guidance,
Allowing the authority
To believe
In the value of
Her title.

Coming to the table as the influencer rather than the authority gives you greater flexibility to work with people. An influencer is a listener with the ability to turn disadvantage to advantage.

We all have the opportunity to be influencers, people willing to affect others with quiet words and actions. Influencers understand people, and they know the many sides to an issue.

Today, be part of influencing what is important to you. Be a listener, and guide with quiet words and actions. Come to the table and begin to make your part of the world better.

July 9

Head and heart—
Leading
Requires
Both,
For the head
Provides the right
Direction
And the
Heart
Hears
What those following
Need
To be inspired
In a new direction.

Balancing logic and emotion can be difficult, as we tend to use one side predominantly. Both head and heart are needed for complete and effective leading in our small part of the world.

Knowing the right direction to take and leading people in that direction are two different skills. Helping others in the transition takes into account what they need, and is done on an individual basis.

As you lead today, use both logic and emotion. Force yourself to think in both ways and to use both thoughtful logic to give you the right direction and intentional emotion and empathy in understanding how this direction affects others' needs.

July 10

Your choices
Express your
Philosophy
Of leading—
Individual
Choice
For a collective.
A leader
Takes the ultimate
Responsibility
For choices
And the impact
Made.

Each day as you lead, you display your philosophy of leadership through the choices you make. Not only the results but also how you get to your choice are part of who you are as a leader.

Whether you are leading as a parent, community member, or boss, your decisions affect those around you. A leader takes responsibility for those choices and their impact on others.

As you begin to understand that you are a leader, take stock of those whom your decisions affect. These may be your children, neighbors, or coworkers. Take responsibility for how your choices affect them. Reflect on how you make decisions, and determine if that matches your leadership philosophy.

July 11

Successful
Leadership
Is not measured
In times of abundance
And ease
But when
Challenges come from
Every corner
And when your
Every decision
Creates controversy,
With people hiding
In cover.
The success of
Putting in place
Courage
Measures a
Leader.

It is when times are tough that leadership is measured and life leaders come forward. During challenging times, leaders are willing to stay involved and work toward solutions.

Leaders are the people who stay the course during controversy. When the situation is difficult, leaders step up and help others meet the challenges. Courage is found in the parent who stays with the struggling teenager. Courage is found in the friend who stays through the illness. And courage is found in the worker who does the right thing when choosing the easy way would make life easier.

Today, think about your own courage to lead in hard times. Your courage may be in your marriage or at work. Are you willing to stand and do the right thing even when the situation becomes difficult? Reflect on the right things to do, and move to do them.

July 12

They knock

Slightly at first

And then

Tap, tap with directness.

A tense face

Is framed by the door,

And small steps in

Remind me

That together,

We can solve any

Problem

As soon as we smile

And believe in

Big steps.

You are a leader the moment someone comes to you for help. In that moment, it is clear that the person knocking at your door has recognized you as a leader. Keep in mind that most of the time, leaders are people who give to others what they need to solve their own problems.

Those with problems, first need their stress lifted, even if slightly. Your helping them balance with a smile will aid in their thinking. Before those with problems can take steps, leaders inspire in them the belief that they can take steps.

Today, believe that you are a leader when people come knocking on your door. *Teacher*, *guide*, and *reflective listener* are all names for a leader. Remember that relieving stress with a smile is important and that your smile tells them a great deal about your leadership. Help them believe.

July 13

Problems are abundant.

Politics swirl in the underground.

The parking lot is hot with

What's wrong.

A lone leader

Begins to talk about

Solutions

In the crowd

Of followers

Engrossed in the problem

And turns one at time

From follower to

New leader.

It is easy to focus on problems, but focusing on problems keeps us from beginning the work needed to solve problems. People engaged in politics and in discussing what's wrong need only one to turn the conversations toward solutions.

Leaders don't engage in focusing on what is wrong. They do spend some time examining the issues, and they definitely talk with those involved, but then they begin to work with others to improve the problem.

Today, listen to those around you who are engrossed in what is wrong. Do they need someone to step toward a solution? Be the person in your family, in your community, and at your place of work to turn from the problem to the solution.

July 14

Small, committed
Group
Engaged
In making better
The place
They call
Home,
Depending on each other
On an unknown
Road,
They rattle
A change
That cannot
Be turned back.

It is important to be committed to making your part of the world better. Although every person can make a difference, a small group of committed people can change the world.

A huge part of leading to make a difference is being part of a group of like-minded people—people with the same passion to make a difference. Even when you are entering unknown territory, amazing things can happen when the right people converge on the same mission.

You have an opportunity to make a huge difference when you connect to people who care about the same issues you do. Connection happens when you engage in the work. The right people connect because they are willing to engage. Reflect on the issues that you care about, and find a place where you can engage in making a difference. There, you will find the small but powerful group who will make a difference with you.

July 15

There is no being

Trapped by another's

Philosophy

Or living through

The thinking of others,

For letting other

Opinions

Drown your

Internal voice

Blocks you

From the courage

To follow your own

Heart, intuition, and voice,

As only you know

Your true vocation and

All else

Is secondary.

It is important to not only listen to your internal voice but also nurture your ability to trust yourself. Listening to other opinions and thinking is positive, but allowing the opinions of others to overshadow your own opinion and thinking will not lead you to your potential.

It takes courage to follow your own lead, but listening to your heart, intuition, and voice will take you down your own path to your true calling, and this is critical to being successful.

Today, think about how you have honored and followed your own philosophy. Have your answered your own calling? Take time today to listen to your internal voice and do what you believe is right.

July 16

Leadership is action,
A committed choice
To move
By engaging others and
Inspiring new
Commitment
To an idea
That has no
Walls,
Only the foundation
Of leadership.

When we have an idea of how things can be better, we have to decide how we can engage those directly affected. Making things better requires each of us to move into action and to be persistent in moving toward the vision with other people.

Moving a vision to a reality takes an idea to reality by continuing to create concrete structures to support the vision and conversation to inspire others to believe. With all kinds of learners, multiple ways are necessary to move others toward the vision.

We all have ideas about making things better. Better families, communities, and workplaces make living joyful. What is your idea for improving one or more of these things, whether that idea is small or large? What actions can you take to make that idea a reality? Start those actions today.

July 17

Clearing the way,

Working

Alongside,

Staying in

The shadow.

Work is done.

And

When they say,

"We did it,"

Leading is

Complete.

Leaders don't always take front and center. At some times and in some places, leadership means clearing the way for others to do their work, the leader in the trenches, working side by side with others.

When a group of people accomplishes difficult work and know they did it, a leader has accomplished great leadership. The leader has left a valuable imprint of accomplishment in those around him or her.

Look at your leadership and determine how often you are front and center and how often you are ensuring that those working with you feel accomplishment. Be determined to give the gift of accomplishment by leading from the back.

July 18

Instilling a
Mental picture
For others
Of what
Was just a
Thought
One morning
But bubbled
In dreams
And doodles
During meetings
Provides purpose
To those needing
A vision.

We all have dreams of making something better—a cause, a workplace, or a relationship. Your ideas that start out as doodles during meetings can be the exact vision needed to make things better.

Instilling a vision that is intangible requires the skill of making an idea a concrete vision—perhaps a model or modeling positive behavior. Think about the senses and how you can use those senses to give form to your idea.

Begin to draw out your idea. Give it structure and then share it with one other person. Provide the mental picture, and you will provide a vision for others.

July 19

Lift those around you

To see what is possible

By raising your own

Standards

Of living and working.

Ensuring that

People

Are inspired

To perform

Everyday tasks

Beyond

Their own perceptions

Of their

Limitations

Is leading.

One of the best ways to inspire others to perform better is to raise your own performance standards in life and work. As you raise your level of performance, be mindful and thoughtful to model a healthy balance.

With balance, we all can go beyond our perceived limits. A leader to model the living needed is required for a better way of doing things to be achieved. Going beyond our perceived limits does not have to be about creating a new cure but can be about performing our everyday tasks to our full potential.

Today, concentrate on raising your level of performance on everyday tasks. Inspire the people in your life to do the same. We will make a difference today.

July 20

There are those
Floating
Through,
Wishing for
A position and
An office with
A window,
But the window
Provides no light,
As courage to
Shine light
Comes from the
Internal window
Of passion,
And it alone
Completes
The vision
While the office
Stays dark.

There are people wishing for an office, a name plate, and power but who are not willing to earn the title of *leader*. Leaders shine light to others no matter where they sit and no matter their titles.

Being willing to share your light with others comes from your passion for the people you work with and the work you do daily. Whether that work is at home or out in the community, leaders use their courage to allow others to shine.

Today, no matter your title or where you sit, have the courage to lead by providing a light to others. Take time to listen to one other person, and encourage their dreams.

July 21

Leadership strength
Is never rude,
And kindness
To others is
Required
While being
Truthful.
Bold action never
Needs bullying.
Active leaders
Have the softer
Characteristics
To make a difference.

Good leaders know that people are the most important resource in any community. Strong leaders are able to be kind while leading and never need to bully others to complete their visions.

Caring about people and using kindness within your family, workplace, and community is a strength. When people know that your care is real, they are more likely to follow your lead.

Reflect today on your own characteristics of leadership and determine if you are kind and caring or if you are more likely to bully to get your way. Determine to be kinder in your leadership and to lead without fear.

July 22

Fence painting

Is fun.

I smile

To ensure

Those on the

Sideline

Begin to feel

My excitement.

One painter and then two.

Yes, they believe

Fence painting

Is fun.

If you approach each day and task with enthusiasm, other people will follow with the same attitude. Even during hard times, people will emulate the leader's attitude and feelings toward the work.

You can share positive energy with those around you by coming to each day with an attitude that says you choose to be there. Projecting a feeling that we can do amazing things together is important in leadership.

Today, help the people around you understand that excitement and a positive attitude are a part of you and that you expect the same excitement them from those you interact with daily. Begin to behave with positive actions, and you will have many people enjoying painting the fence.

July 23

Give gratitude

To your critics,

Those uncomfortable

And willing

To complain,

At times slashing

At you personally,

For they offer

You insight

And opportunity

To transition

Them

Or to use

Their thinking

In your

Teaching.

With gratitude,

Thank your critics.

Those people who disagree with your ideas or provide insight into how you are communicating your vision provide you a powerful gift. Listening to their opinions may not change your course, but it does provide an opportunity to make adjustments.

There are people you will never win over, but they may provide information to help you avoid stumbling blocks or a way to reach others influenced by them.

Our critics provide a service to us by allowing us to see inside another way of viewing issues or even ourselves. Take a moment to give gratitude to those brave enough to provide the insight. Listen to the critics and then proceed with enlightenment.

July 24

Life is filled
With complicated
Issues,
Pros and cons
That never point to
A simple solution.
It is a chaotic,
Fast-paced,
Ever-changing platform.
One who can
Calm the chaos
Long enough
To make it simpler
For others,
Cut through
The debate,
And provide the road
Is a leader.

Life is complicated. Leaders at home and work are people who can cut through the chaos and help others work through problems by removing the barriers and distractions.

It is difficult to keep focused on the right stuff and to disregard the ever-swirling mass of unproductive verbiage and behaviors. Good leaders have the ability to cut a path through that because they don't get engaged in unproductive activities.

Today, reflect on how you respond to the unproductive activity around you and to the people you care about each day. Make sure you are not engaged in those activities, and then begin to help others keep focused on the important work.

July 25

Learning with those

You serve,

Being open to

New ideas,

Especially the ideas

Of others,

Encourages

And engages

New visions

Of places

Never thought

Possible

Until learning sparked

A light.

To keep a vision fresh and alive, a leader must be open to learning. Being open to new ideas and thoughts allows us to see new possibilities.

Learning can take many forms, but it actively seeks out information through activity and people, and by quiet observation of the world around us. Learning may take place in the class that you have always wanted to take or in the class you have been afraid to take.

Take some time to reflect on your learning, and determine a course to expose yourself to new ideas and new ways of looking at the world. Be a learner today.

July 26

Arranging and rearranging,
Telling others she is
Responsible
For the full load,
And feeling each stressful
And strategized move,
Management abounds
While a nurturer of the spirit
And enhancer of abilities
Guides,
Sharing the load,
Feels the pieces
Fall into place,
And
Leads others.

There is a difference between managing tasks and leading those in your immediate community. This holds true in your dealings with family, friends, and coworkers.

Leading ensures that the task is done while the spirit of others is nurtured. Leaders leave tasks done and people better by allowing learning and growth.

Today, think about your willingness to lead others by sharing your load and guiding others to enhance their abilities. The tasks you have will get done eventually, but today, make sure you leave the people around you better.

July 27

Cubicle watchers

Hear words

And examine paper,

But they define

Leaders

Through eyes

That watch

What happens

Before and after

Doors close.

The alignment

Of words, paper, and

Action is easy to

Spot.

Those unaligned

Pass through,

Leading no one.

People around you watch your actions and compare them with your words. Your actions are powerful and affect who will follow you. Your actions can inspire others to change their own actions.

When your personal behaviors don't align with your words, you have no possibility of making a lasting impact. Being aware of your own words and actions is the first step to making sure you are worthy of being watched.

Examine your words and actions for alignment. Are you living what you believe and what you tell others is important? Begin to take each day to closely examine your actions and realign when needed.

July 28

One final test
To look back
To see
If
Those left
Behind
Carry forward
New goals
With the
Conviction
And passion
Left by a
Past leader.

When you have moved on and take a look back, you see major change in your work. This is the normal process. When you look back, look at the people you have left, and their ability to thrive and work with passion. Are they carrying forward, doing the right thing?

Programs, rules, and work will change, but the people are a leader's legacy. People are the lasting impact we make when we lead. Those important lessons about integrity, caring, and growing others is what will last when you're gone.

Reflect on what you are providing the people around you. Think about one lesson you want to make sure is passed to those important to you. Begin to develop a plan to ensure that this lasts after you are gone.

July 29

Gaining strength

Courage, and confidence

Each time

An experience

Allows you to face

Fear

With straight-on

Abandon

Knowing

With one look

You must do

The one thing

You think is

Impossible

Then

Possible.

Unless you are willing to face fear, you never know your full potential. When you meet the tasks you fear impossible with courage and confidence, suddenly, the impossible becomes possible.

It only takes one person willing to face her or his fear and then turn to help others face their fear to get us on the road to possibility. Sometimes when we deem something impossible, our biggest fear is simply that we will fail.

Facing fear allows us to think beyond failing and to think of possibility. Today, reflect on what you are afraid to attempt. Face the fear with an openness to examine it, and work to determine possible ways to overcome what you fear.

July 30

You give a gift
Of learning
When they
Determine how best
To get things
Done after
Clear vision
Of what needs to
Happen.
People will
Surprise
You
With their
Power of imagination
And creativity
While
Feeling valued.

Effective leaders allow others to learn by doing, even if it means things get done in a way the leader would not do them. Providing the opportunity for those around you to determine how to best do the assigned task offers them a chance to learn and to develop a lifelong ability to solve issues.

It is often easier, and perhaps more satisfying, to do by yourself because it is done exactly as you would like, but the gift of learning is a precious gift that changes people. It allows them to use their creativity and gives the gift of value.

Today, think about giving others the opportunity to learn. Push those you are in contact with to learn. They may not be used to using their creativity to solve problems, but encourage them to solve the issues at hand. Plan a learning activity for those in your circle. Be a teacher today.

July 31

It is not given,

Not purchased

With a degree.

It is earned

Daily

By serving

Those around you

With care,

By providing a vision

Of something better,

And by inspiring

Others to follow

In your footsteps,

Not once in a while but

Day in and day out,

With gratitude

That you are given

The opportunity.

To lead.

Leadership is a daily activity. No title or degree makes you a leader. Leadership is earned each day in how you live your life.

Leaders earn the title of leader by serving those around them. A leader is willing to stop and give meaning to the possibility of making our world better, even if it is a small part of the world. Earning a leadership role will require inspiration and the ability to motivate others to better themselves and their surroundings every day.

Don't be afraid of leading or of earning a leadership role. Engage in serving and in sharing your vision of what would make your corner of the world better. Model for others what is right, and make a commitment to start each day with this in mind. Then you will have earned the title of leader.

August

Forgiveness is a process that requires both thought and action. Forgiveness is essential to living a life filled with opportunity. Withholding forgiveness blocks your potential and eventually makes you unable to see opportunity.

To forgive, you must release the anger you feel over personal mistakes and hurtful situations. Releasing happens with an awareness that there is a need and then by creating the words and actions to let go of negative thoughts and feelings.

This month, we spend time on examining the forgiveness process, including our capacity to forgive ourselves, others, and hurtful situations by reframing how we look at them. Take this time to work on healing yourself, those you love, and those you know.

August Focuses

Forgiveness is an active process.

Forgiving heals your mind, body, and spirit.

Forgiveness opens you to possibility.

August 1

Forgiveness,

A release of the

Heart is

The gift

The contribution

The offering

You

Willingly

Provide to

Your conscience

In order to

Gift, contribute, and offer

More to the world.

Although people think of giving forgiveness to others, the true gift or forgiveness is to yourself. When you hold back forgiveness, you are filled with negative emotions that keep you from moving forward.

Releasing through forgiveness is freeing to your heart and allows you to be open to new opportunity. It is your gift to yourself to make yourself and your surroundings better.

Today, determine what you are holding on to and have not been able to forgive. You may need to forgive someone else or maybe yourself. Begin the process of forgiving. Start by saying who you forgive and what are you forgiving. Repeat your forgiveness statement regularly.

August 2

Authentic forgiveness
Liberates your
Mind and heart
From being captured
By negativity
And self-destructive
Thoughts
And releases
You
To new possibilities.

Freedom is granted to those who make the choice to forgive. Holding on to negative thoughts of others or yourself will keep you caught in a self-destructive cycle.

When you release negativity from your heart, you begin to be open to possibilities and potential that have been missing from your everyday life.

Forgiving is not easy, and it is both a mental and physical activity. It often does not happen in a single moment but happens because we decide to work at releasing those feelings that have been hurting us mentally and physically. Today, take time to center your mind, body, and spirit on the release of a situation that causes you pain. Use your words and breathe to release the pain. Work at repeating the words and finding the places in your body that are keeping you back.

August 3

To hold on to
Resentment
Is to stay
Underwater
Only watching
The surface.
As long as we
Hold ourselves
Under,
We lack fresh
Breath
And
Willingly suffocate
Rather than
Break the surface
To breathe
Large gulps
Of hope.

Gulps of hope are available to each one of us with the courage to reach out and break the surface. Each time you feel that underwater feeling reach and break the surface.

Providing fresh breath to your mind, body, and soul is replenishing and nourishing. It allows you to remove your barriers and to believe in the hope of a better life for yourself and others.

Use today to break the surface of those fears or barriers keeping you from full potential. When you breathe in the hope, let go of resentment. Tell a friend about your courage.

August 4

The past cannot
Change
What we carry and
Does not change
The pictures
Of the past.
Forgiveness
Of self and others
Cannot
Change
The past,
But
It does
Enlarge the
Potential of the
Future.

When we are unwilling to release mistakes or past transgressions, we are choosing to live in the past rather than move forward into the future. Although we cannot change the past, we don't have to allow it to create our future.

To ensure that we are placing ourselves in place for maximum potential, we have to let go of anger, resentment, and bitterness. As long as those feelings are within us, an engaging future is out of reach.

Today, search for those negative feelings that you are still living with, and determine to release them from your mind and body. Refuse to live in the past, and choose to live in an engaging life.

August 5

The first step
To meeting
Your full
Life potential
Engages you
In full release
Of all
Past mistakes
While embedding
The lesson
In your daily
Life walk.
Begin with one
Step.

Human potential is a precious and often wasted resource. Past mistakes that you hold onto and revisit with shame hold you back from fulfilling your potential.

Learning from mistakes is important, but reliving mistakes by continuing to think about them is dangerous. Take what you have learned and then let the mistakes no longer take up your time or energy.

Take the first step to let go of those images and memories holding you back. You may do this by meditating on or journaling words of release. Talk to someone about your release to make it real for you. Take your first step today.

August 6

Humanness is filled

With amazing

Flashes of

Brilliance

And moments

Of throbbing painful

Missteps in character.

The choice to forgive

The missteps

In character

Touches the core

Of humanity

And changes the course

Of who you

Are.

Although we all make mistakes and even repeat our missteps in character, each person is worthy of forgiveness, even those who have hurt us. When you are able to move past the painful moments, you begin the process of positively changing the very core of your being. The process of forgiving requires a desire to improve who you are and begins the slow change.

When we are able to forgive ourselves, we have the skills to forgive others. This is not forgetting and moving on but is about reflecting on actual internal change. Whether the change is an internal improvement or a letting go of anger and hurt, it focuses on positive energies. Forgiveness is a process.

There is no better day than to today to begin changing the course of who you are by removing negative missteps and replacing them with positive thinking and possibility of improvement. Forgive one of your own missteps in character, and develop a list of helpful and positive reminders to keep you from repeating the misstep. If you are holding anger, release it by forgiving the situation that made you angry.

August 7

I am held
Hostage
By intense
Emotion
That chokes
Me with tears.
I am fearful
Of release
For I am unsure
I will recover
From the rush of
This intense
Encompassing
Feeling,
And so it leaks
With slow painful
Spurts
Into my life and
The lives of those
I love.
I long for release.

When you hold on to intense emotions for fear of being overrun by them and unable to stop them, you are hurting your mind, body, and spirit. Releasing intense negative emotions can be scary, but it is a fear we must face.

It is important that you know you will not break and that you are resilient enough to recover. To release by talking through with a friend or by allowing the tears to come, you have to first know that you will recover.

Do not be held hostage by negative thinking and feeling. Begin to know that you are stronger than these emotions. Think about how you need to begin the process of release. Know that you are strong.

August 8

I felt my body
Turn inward
With surging pain,
Drying with a
Crinkle
Until
Quenching
My soul in
Kindness,
Giving words of
Love
To myself,
Recognizing still
The mistake,
But releasing
The pain
I know can
Fill my body with
Life again.

Each person is responsible for filling their bodies and souls with forgiveness. Forgiving yourself is a powerful force in living a well-balanced and fully engaged life.

When you are unable to forgive yourself, you are unable to forgive others. Without the ability to forgive, your body, mind, and spirit will surge with pain.

Today, take time to intentionally provide yourself with the kindness of forgiving the mistakes or lapses in character from your past. This process and attitude must be practiced daily. Write down what you need to forgive, and post it somewhere to remind yourself to repeat the forgiveness daily.

August 9

Forgiving is

Not forgetting

But

Creating a new way

To remember—

A way that

Does not

Set tears

Or damage

A loving spirit

But finds a

Way to love

All with

Inclusiveness

Of past, present, and future.

One of the most powerful gifts of forgiveness is that it can create in you new ways to look at people and situations. Forgiveness is not about forgetting that something bad happened but about being able to remember in a way that gives positive energy to you and those around you.

When we begin to work at forgiving, we open the door to reframe how we feel about and look at an issue. We decide to take back any power, that the situation had over us. In taking power back, we then have the ability to learn and to be inclusive with our experiences without fear.

Choose an experience that is hurting you and begin to brainstorm how you might be able to look at this situation in a new way. When you find a new way to look at the situation, decide if this new way gives you positive energy. Talk with a close friend about your new way of looking at the situation. This is a start to forgiveness.

August 10

Head bowed

In reverent prayer

I ask for

The larger spirit

To give me the wisdom

To remember

Each painful

Lesson

In order

To omit

Repeating

And

To give me the mercy

To move forward

Without renewing

Each scar.

Asking for wisdom to not repeat mistakes is an important part of moving forward. Another part of moving forward is making changes in your thinking and actions. Those changes are what help you to not repeat a mistake again.

Although lessons need to be remembered, they need to be reframed so we do not relive them in our thoughts and create more hurt. This can be difficult but is doable. When we are intentional in our thinking, we work to ensure that our learning from our mistakes and not creating more hurt.

Today, take time to be reflective in prayer and ask for both wisdom and mercy. Find one mistake you can learn from and begin to look at the mistake as learning. Remove the hurts associated with the mistake. Soak in your wisdom and dole out your mercy.

August 11

Tolerant

Of each violation

Of my own instinct

At the end

Of each

Day

I am aware

Of the lapses

In thoughtful living.

Tolerant

Because I continue

To be mindful of

An improved morning,

The restart of

A possible

Improvement.

When you are aware that you have the ability to start anew each day and can work toward living a thoughtful life, you are in the forgiveness journey. It is important to be tolerant with yourself when you fail to live up to your standards.

Being tolerant means not reliving each transgression but creating a change in your thoughts and actions. Being tolerant allows you to forgive yourself and to accept that you are a good person who makes mistakes. It also allows you to see tolerance and forgiveness in other people.

Be tolerant with yourself and be the first person to believe you are good. When you restart each day, start with a plan to improve what needs to be better. Make the plan easy enough to follow for one day, and then follow it the next day.

August 12

My teacher

Walks with me

In forgiveness

While teaching

Me

A better way

To move through

The maze of

Life.

When I fall

My teacher

With shaking head

Smiles

And offers

A hand

To pull me forward.

We walk in

Order for me

To one day

Teach.

We all have teachers who help us when we fall. I call on many teachers but often call on my higher spirit to help me forgive myself and others.

When you call on your teachers and they help you, there is an expectation that you will teach forward what you have learned and will lend your hand to those who call on you. The best teachers are removed from blaming or assigning guilt.

Calling on your teachers for help is healthy. If you need help, make the call, whether it is on the phone or in prayer. Take your teacher's hand, and then take your turn as the teacher and extend your own hand in teaching.

August 13

Truth

Clear

Unless

Forgiveness

Is given

To yourself

And the situation

Is closed.

Movement forward

Requires forgiveness

For you

To find

Truth

Clear.

Granting forgiveness to yourself is often one of the most difficult things you do, and one of the most important. To close the door on a bad situation or moment in a healthy manner, you must incorporate that situation or moment into your being with forgiveness.

When you incorporate mistakes or hurtful moments, you have determined to see the hurt or mistake in a different way. A path reframing it into an opportunity or learning.

Today, open the door to your mistakes or to those situations that have been hurtful. Stop avoiding them, and bring them inside in order to reframe them into opportunities for learning or for moving forward. Choose just one issue and give it a try.

August 14

The weight is heavy
It pulls my heart
And spirit
Down.
Determined to
Be free,
I must
Release the weight,
So I let go
With a breath to
The skies,
Allowing heart and spirit
To soar,
With the weight
Falling
Without me.

When you carry emotional weight, your heart and spirit are affected, along with your everyday living. The negativity can eventually drag you down unless you have the courage and persistence to let it go.

Releasing weight that you have carried for a long time can feel scary. Releasing it in a healthy manner may require help from a higher being. Raise your thoughts to the sky or send them to the earth, asking for help.

Today, recognize an emotional weight you are carrying. Release it through breathing deeply and letting go of the weight through your breath. Use your words to tell your body to emancipate yourself from the emotional burden. Releasing the burden may take time, so repeat as often as needed.

August 15

Release
And accept the realization
That people
Pass into
Your history
Even when loved
The release
Removes them
From your future.
With lingering
Grief,
You step into
Your destiny.

When you let go of emotional trauma, you may realize that there will be people who need to pass into your history because you can no longer carry them and be healthy.

Allowing even someone you love to move to your history is a healthy part of forgiveness and of moving forward. You can grieve the adjustment, but those in your history are not lost; they have simply changed their place.

Today, step into your destiny by acknowledging those people who need to be moved to your history. Say good-bye by writing a letter to yourself indicating why it is time to let go and move on to a new way of living. Know that you can honor the person and time you spent together and still move forward.

August 16

Tears pour
And spend
Every emotion,
And finally ,
Forgiveness
Settles in
As
Learning lingers
On edge.
Tears continue
To soak
Into a future
And a hope of happiness.

Tears are often an important part of release. Allowing the flow of tears can help you move through forgiveness, but you need to work with your words and thoughts to shift from grief to living in the present and looking forward to your future.

Forgiveness is an emotional process. Those emotions can be avoided when you bury them, but buried hurts have a way of resurfacing over and over again. We have to face hurt to get over it.

Today, face a hurt that you continue to bury. Allow your emotions to surround the hurt. It can be scary, but this is an important part of being able to move toward happiness.

August 17

Bridges demolished

Paths overgrown

No footprint

Left to retrace

And no other

Choice

But to move

Leading, living, loving

Forward

To a new day

To a new stage

And work

For

A forward future.

Sometimes, there is no return and no other choice but to move forward. Although there is no way back, you can honor the past for the gifts it provided your future.

Move forward by leading, living, and loving rather than turning backward. This means letting go of those people, places, and histories and look forward.

Are you holding on to people and places in your life even though it is time to honor and let go of them? Today, take time to honor the gifts given by the experience of knowing them, and then write a good-bye letter for yourself. End the letter with a description of how your future will look in the coming weeks and year.

August 18

Everyone owns
A history
A past
That imparts a
Bias
And wisdom,
But living in
Your past
Cannot
Equal
Your future
Potential.

Having a past is much different than living in the past. Each person's past is filled with good and bad memories, but the past is something we need to learn from and then let go.

To live full and engaged lives, we have to be present in our current lives. Being present in your current life means forgiving the parts of your past that may be holding you back.

Today, reflect on your past and determine if you are holding yourself back by wishing you were still in a past situation or wishing you could change a part of your past. With intention, say good-bye and work to keep the situation out of your thoughts by keeping your thoughts on your present and future.

August 19

Those holding

On with

Full strength

Or just to

Scraps.

Believe

The past

Is the only

Future.

Release of

Ended

Accomplishments,

Relationships,

And periods of life

Is knowing there

Is a future.

Holding on to past accomplishments, relationships, or times can keep us from moving forward and finding new opportunities.

Understanding that you can honor the past but cannot hold on to it is essential to being present in your life. We can hold on to both positive and negative areas of our past. We need to let go of both positive and negative to meet our potential. When we are able to be free of our past, we are open to opportunities.

Today, reflect on what you are holding on to from your past, good or bad. Release it with persistence daily until it is only a learned lesson or a good memory. You will know you are there when you begin to find new opportunities and take them.

August 20

Wisdom learned
From our history
Stays
Within our being.
Time allowing
Breathing to push out
The vivid
Images that feed
Our grudges and fears
Which held our spirit
Hostage in the
Same spot
And our
Wisdom stagnant.

We gain wisdom from our histories, but we must rid ourselves of those images that feed our grudges and fears. Those images, real or imagined, hold our spirits back from meeting their potential.

We start releasing the images by facing them. When such an image comes into your thoughts, stay with it and examine it without emotion.

Today, think about images you are replaying that feed your anger or hurt. Face the images and then begin to create a new visual that feeds you in a positive and healthy way. Do not let negative images take over your thinking.

August 21

Performing

Autopsy

On a living spirit

In order

To determine

Who or what is wrong

Ends with unnecessary

Pain.

Letting go

Of what went

Wrong

Allows energies

To move forward

Toward the

Solutions,

Free of

Hurt.

Finding who is wrong and proving it is unproductive. The process of proving right or wrong is painful and does not move us toward healing. Putting energy toward positive solutions heals everyone.

It can be difficult to avoid the trap of performing an autopsy on a living spirit. Proving we are right may give us a temporary feeling of power, but it is not positive power.

Working with solutions and allowing each person to find his or her own right or wrong provides a win for all. Today, consider a time when you completed an autopsy to prove you were right, and take time to give healing words to the person whom you tried to prove was not right. The next time you want to be right, redirect your thinking to a solution.

August 22

The nights
When I am unsure
Of faith, hope, and love—
Nights
Of holding on to
Anger and fear—
I determine
With palms
Turned to
One higher,
Allowing myself
To be
Carried and held
And the earth
Surrounds me
In care.
My eyes
Open to light
And renewed
Faith, hope, and love.

Faith, hope, and love provide a foundation to authentic and meaningful forgiveness. All three are the ingredients for a life with the capability to be lived fully.

Believing that you can forgive and be forgiven is the first step to being free to be open to your future. Having hope for a better future allows us to take the next step toward new opportunity, and love is the one feeling necessary to move forward.

Today, take stock in your sense of faith, hope, and love. Nurture each of these powerful actions and make sure you have all three in balance. Talk to a friend about the one you feel least secure with, and determine some steps to strengthen it.

August 23

My body

Betrayed my

Mind and heart

By rendering

My fingers and toes

Unmovable

And slowing my organs

To a stop.

My forgiveness for

This offense

Is difficult

To provide,

But I determine

To surround my body

With kindness

And forgive

The transgression

To live in balance.

Graceful aging is difficult as your body gives way to the ailments of your grandmother. Part of living in grace is providing your body with kindness and forgiving the transgressions of illness and age.

We all begin to recognize that the precious shells we have been working in all these years are slowing down. This often feels like a betrayal because our minds and hearts still feel young.

Find time to give gratitude for all of the things your body is still able to do. Be amazed at how your body has supported you all these years. Fill your body with breath to provide health and care. Forgive and accept where your body is today.

August 24

If you

Recognize

How precious

Your life is,

That time is

Limited and

Pain in life

Happens,

That your actions

Have awesome

Power—

If you have

This knowledge,

You will increase

Successful

Forgiveness.

We cannot avoid that our time here is limited or that we all experience pain during our lifetime, but we can control how we act and react during our short lifetime. Realizing the power of our actions can lead to changing ourselves and our environment.

Every action we perform has the power to hurt or heal. Being aware of this power is one of the keys to forgiving fully. Although our words are important, what we put into action and how we change our behaviors provide needed energy and give life to forgiveness.

Today, think about the actions you want to put into play. Be aware of your power to hurt and heal with each action, and choose healing. Step forward and do what is needed today.

August 25

I walk the water's
Edge,
Waves crashing,
Sweeping away to
Clean the sand.
I look out to the horizon,
Seeing the ocean's vastness
And never-ending power,
And wonder,
Is it the all-encompassing
Power or the
Repeating waves
That are able to forgive
All human mistakes?
I wish to be all-encompassing
And repeating
In order
To fill my life
With waters of forgiveness.

A larger view of the world helps us focus on what is really important. There are things that are important enough to take a firm stand on, but sometimes we get focused on things that are not that important.

Along with having a larger view, we need to be as persistent as the repeating waves to cleanse our minds and spirits of negative thoughts. Forgiveness is a repeating process and, depending on the situation, can take time. We have to stay with the process.

Both the larger view and persistence are necessary for you to be present in forgiving yourself, others, and difficult situations. Think about an issue that you are currently struggling with, and determine if you need to look at the larger view. Is this issue worthy of your core values? Is it something that needs you to be more persistent in forgiving? Work on your findings as you answer the questions.

August 26

Authentic

Forgiveness is

When you have

Moved from

Anger

To appreciation

For the learning

And you know

You are better

Because you had

The experience.

Anger gone

Gratitude embedded.

You may need to repeat the process of forgiveness until you feel no anger. The day you can appreciate what you learned from the experience, you know you have completed the process of forgiveness.

Depending on the situation, forgiveness may take time, but working through the anger and hurt can eventually lead to learning and to becoming a better person. This is worth working toward daily.

Reflect on a situation requiring forgiveness and begin the process of forgiving yourself, someone else, or the situation. Realizing that there is a benefit from the situation may help you move the process forward. Take today to appreciate all the learning you have had this year.

August 27

Forgiveness is not

Forgetting

But releasing

The tight grip

Choking you

And others.

The release

Allows a

Surge of life

With the will to

Go forward.

Reconciliation will

Require

Authentic change

In both

Hearts and hands.

Authentic forgiveness can release the grip on your life that is blocking your potential. Several changes in your daily living occur once you release with forgiveness.

When you forgive, it isn't that you forget but that you no longer give those feelings of anger power over how you see life or live life. Forgiveness does not mean automatic reconciliation but does open the door to reconciliation if changes in thinking and living are made.

Release the grip that is holding you back from positive living, and begin the process of forgiving. Understand that changes must happen in yourself and the person or situation that you are forgiving before there can be reconciliation.

August 28

Healing ourselves and

Those around us

Is our most

Important contribution

To our

World, community, and family.

There is

No healing

Without the

Practice of

Forgiveness,

Which must

Be rehearsed

And repeated

Throughout

Each day of

Each life.

Forgiveness not only heals us powerfully but also provides healing to our world, community, and family. It is perhaps the most important contribution we make to improving the world.

To begin the healing process, we make the choice to forgive hurt. You can't forgive or heal without facing and feeling the pain. We may avoid forgiveness because we don't want to face the pain again.

The practice of forgiveness includes concentrating on the hurt by breathing it in and transforming it into positive energy with an exhale. Continue to do this until you feel that the experience has been transformed to a positive one. Define forgiveness as your contribution to the world today.

August 29

By the grace
Of the light,
I stand at
Life's chalkboard,
Marking
Thoughts and actions,
Giving a day's
Worth of
Intersecting thoughts
With some missteps
That during the
Darkness of night
Are wiped clean
Enough
For one more day
Of chalking.

Life is like a chalkboard. You spend time making your marks, and although the marks are not permanent, the marks are never completely gone. Each day, you have the courage to make your mark, and each night you know that you have the opportunity to forgive the mistakes.

Keep in mind that forgiveness is an action and requires a change. The bigger the mistake, the more action and change required, and the more the marks stay on the board as a reminder.

It is important to have the courage to stand at the board and make a mark. Being afraid to make a mark because of a mistake is self-defeating. Each evening, after a day of marking, reflect on the actions you need to take to correct mistakes. Begin the process of correcting those mistakes—perhaps through an apology or a change in how you approach things.

August 30

Life is an adventure
In forgiveness
Because each journey
Fills with moments of
Minor and major
Thoughtless actions
That must be
Approached with
The enthusiasm of
Every new adventure
In order to
Engage in a
Vibrant way
Of living.

An adventure is an undertaking requiring effort. An adventure is also exciting, and it brings you to places you never knew you could go. Like an adventure, forgiveness requires effort and brings us to unknown places.

Take on forgiveness like you take on new adventure—with some excitement and enthusiasm. The adventure of forgiveness will bring you unfamiliar emotional and physical changes. This adventure will create engagement in life and put possibility in front of you.

Open yourself to going on a needed adventure of forgiveness. Know that it will take you to places you have not been. Adventures need preparation, so begin preparing. Think about a person or situation you can begin a forgiveness adventure with today. Take the adventure on with excitement, and be ready to go new places.

August 31

My heart opens
To the possibility
Of forgiveness
Offered to
Me.
I know in
Accepting the
Grace provided,
Changes in
Thinking and acting
Must be embedded
In my living
And
My own forgiveness
Must mirror
The gift provided.

When you are offered forgiveness, you are given a gift that provides healing to you and the person offering it. Accepting the forgiveness of someone else is powerful and allows you to find full possibility in your life.

Accepting forgiveness has meaning only when you are able to accomplish two things: acknowledging that you are worthy and changing your thoughts and actions. Forgiving yourself and changing your actions are big steps to beginning to accept forgiveness.

To be able to accept forgiveness, you will want to ready your heart, so today, reflect on how you accept forgiveness and whether you acknowledge that you are worthy of forgiveness and can make changes in your thoughts and behaviors. Find the right words to help yourself to accept forgiveness, and use them daily.

September

The month of September focuses on tapping your courage to live a complete life while being true to yourself. Courage to live a full life requires reflection, opening you to the world and centering you in the positive.

A life of courage will lead you to periodically question your life and its purpose. It will have you take thoughtful risks and practice the courage to be resilient as you keep going. The questioning continues through your life, as you are a work in progress.

It takes courage to live your path authentically even when your journey does not mirror that of the rest of your family or community. Being true to your values and vision regardless of what others may think is a key to courage.

September Focuses

Fully engage in your life.

Be yourself.

Apply courage thoughtfully.

September 1

Courage to live
Authentically
With your
Vision,
With your
Core values,
Is a mission
In daily
Living
And self-
Correcting
To stay
Authentic
With courage.

All people have visions of what is possible as they live their daily lives. Most people never engage enough courage to participate in the possible but rather live on the edge of safety.

Working within your core values to begin moving your vision to reality requires one step at a time, walking toward the goal until it is reached even if that takes a long time. You make a daily commitment to keep on track.

On the first day of September, begin to live in courage. Visualize your dream and take your first step to making courage part of your daily commitment.

September 2

Live bravely
And allow
Yourself to risk,
Knowing chance
Is an opportunity,
A way to grow
And develop
Your mind, body, and spirit.
Bravery
Is the road
To finding
Who you can
Be.

It takes a great deal of courage to be yourself every day. Take time to slow down, develop your mind, body, and spirit to capacity, and then be brave enough to fulfill your personal potential in the world. This is true freedom.

With many pressures to follow the current trend, it is easy to lose who you are. We often don't fit the pictures that others have created for us. It takes courage to surface yourself and find joy in your own gifts.

Find time today to spend with yourself and listen to who you are and what is important to you. Risk putting that person out to another during the week. This is the first step toward living bravely with who you are.

September 3

Living authentically

By opening

Yourself

And being

Comfortable

With who you

Are

Allows you to

Put yourself

Out to the world

For discovery

And to make a

Difference in

The world.

Living your life with your values and decisions in alignment creates a freedom to put yourself out into the world to make a difference. This happens when you are comfortable with yourself and are able to provide for others what you value.

When you live with the courage to value yourself and your passions, you have the opportunity to make your home, workplace, and community better. It takes a brave person to put into our world what is truly valued.

Today, be thoughtful about what you are willing to put out into the world. Be reflective. Is what you are putting out into the world your authentic self? Work at being brave enough to share yourself with those you love and those you lead.

September 4

Each life is a privilege
Given to us
To live
Fully
With the
Courage
To
Engage in honoring
The person
You were born
To be
And the courage
To live life
As you were
Intended.

The life given to you is a privilege, a daily opportunity to improve yourself and your surroundings. While we are in a continual improvement cycle, being grounded and aware of who we are and honoring what we were meant to do takes courage.

Honoring what you are meant to do means listening to your heart and head. It often means that you will not make everyone happy but will bravely walk your own path.

Today, listen to your heart and head, and determine if you are doing what was intended for your life. Are you walking another's path? If you need to find your own path, help yourself to move in that direction by writing down your intended path. Talk to someone about your path.

September 5

Courage
And patience
Together
Face
Uncertainty.
Waiting
Out the
Doubt,
Listening for
Wisdom
And pausing
For the
Right time to
Move
Engages both
Courage and patience.

Courage and patience are bound together. Without patience, courage may simply be foolishness. Those willing to commit to a passion must exercise patience in order to use courage to move things forward.

Waiting for the right time, the right place, the right people can take as much courage as moving forward. The practice of staying still in your mind helps ensure that you courageously implement the right plan.

Work on your patience while building your courage moves your passion forward. Know that moving forward also takes knowing when to be still and when to listen.

September 6

Alive with knowing,
All human life
Is rare and
Unrepeatable.
Living with
Known and unknown
Purposes
Mandates a
Philosophy of
Courage
To protect
Each life
With reverent,
Respectful action
Each day.

Courageous people live every day by acting in a manner that shows respect to every life. Those who live this way are bold people. It is difficult to live this way with the people we love, and it is especially difficult to live life with the philosophy that all life deserves your care.

We are all unrepeatable, and we all bring a purpose for living. It is hard when you don't know the purpose of another and when that person seems to bring pain to others. The philosophy of honoring each life doesn't mean we have to keep company with people who are negative, but it does mean that we need to value the worth of each person and acknowledge that we don't know the purpose that each brings to world.

Today, spend a quiet moment discovering your own philosophy of honoring people—even those you have trouble dealing with or who make you angry. How can you protect each life you encounter today?

September 7

Life is a short

Span of time,

An undetermined

Moment.

Realizing and

Facing that life ends

Gives an urgent

Understanding

That stepping forward

For yourself

And for others

Is not enough

But obligates

Us to keep

Long strides

And journey

Into the unknown

Before our time

Ends.

When we realize that the time we have on this journey is limited, we begin to understand the urgency to make a difference. Living with courage to take full advantage of every moment requires that we do more than just step up for others but that we be willing to journey with them.

We often avoid the idea that our time is limited. Embracing the idea that time is precious can help us get more done. It sometimes takes courage to face this idea, but once we have faced it, we understand that we have to do more to make a positive difference.

Take time to be comfortable with the idea of your limited time on earth, and reflect on how you want to maximize your actions to make a difference. Ponder your next steps to living every moment to its full potential.

September 8

It is the

Awesome power of

One willing to

Act

That moves

Our world to a

Better place

And models

For others

To shift to doing,

Creating courage

In living.

Courageous actions have the power to move a world, community, neighborhood, or family. A courageous action does not have to be something that makes you famous but something that makes a difference to another person. Being a model for that person provides the example that courage can make a difference in our lives.

Creating an environment of courageous living is the willingness to move forward on an idea. It models for others that being willing to take action is beneficial; we can live our dreams and meet our goals if we act.

Reflect on your own willingness to bravely act in your own part of the world. How are you currently a role model for the power of action in our world? Today, take one action you know makes a difference.

September 9

My heart feels

Broken

And I determine

Suffering and hurting

Are part of living

A full life.

Accepting and facing,

I select

Not the

Suffering

But the

Courage

To feel

The brokenness

And then

Break into

Being

Courageously happy

As another part

Of living.

There is no avoiding pain in life. Pain is part of living. When you can stop avoiding the pain and face it, you are living with courage. Facing your hurt is part of healing and is needed to move your life forward.

It may seem counterproductive to face a feeling you have been avoiding, but the fear of facing pain is as crippling as the pain itself. Until you face the pain, you are selecting suffering.

Build your courage to face a past hurt that you have avoided. Move toward and through the hurt. Know that with courage, you can move beyond the hurt and it cannot hold you captive any longer.

September 10

Fear surrounds and
Fills
Me.
Unable to
Move.
The fear stretches
And
I am sure
It will
Cover me.
I dare
To allow myself
To be covered
And
Discover at
Its worst
I still stand,
Shaking.
I no longer
Give fear
Power
To still
Me.

Fear is a powerful emotion. It can leave us unable to move forward. Everyone experiences fear and fearful situations, but some of us face our fear rather than hide from it.

We often try to avoid our fears by running from them, but it may be more productive to stop and face them. Facing fear allows you to examine what is blocking you from moving forward. By taking a look at your fear up close, you can take away its power.

Take time to reflect on those areas of fear that have the power to change your life. Pick one fear to face today. Facing your fear is the hardest part. Once you have taken on your fear, take it apart and look at it without emotion. Keep facing and examining it until it holds no power over you.

September 11

Courage knows
When to stand
Firm
And
When to
Run,
For there
Are times when
Every fiber of
Courage
Is needed
To turn
In flight
To save
Your internal
Voice
And your own
Road.

Courage isn't always about standing your ground. Sometimes it takes a great deal of courage to walk away. Taking this kind of courageous step often hurts hearts, but when we know it is right, we should walk, perhaps even run, away.

To honor your own voice and keep on your path, it is necessary at times to leave those you love. This is difficult, but your voice and path must be protected and encouraged to grow.

Take time today to reflect on your own voice and path. What are you doing to ensure that you are growing and healthy? If you need to walk away from a situation or person, visualize how that would look, and perhaps talk to a friend to help you begin a new plan.

September 12

Much of
The clash
In our daily
Living
Exists
Because
Alignment to
Our true selves
And purpose
Is disoriented
And there is
Disorder
That only
The genuine
Part of who
We are
Can
Straighten.

Each day contains a struggle to have the courage to live in alignment with our purpose and with our values. When we feel out of sync, it is often because our actions and words are not in alignment with the core of who we are.

Allowing your values to emerge is powerful and sets your daily life on a productive path. The best part of this is that you are able to accomplish what you believe are the right things.

Become still and quiet in the moment and picture your genuine self. Listen to your authentic self to determine what you value. Question yourself to see if you are putting those values into your daily life. If not, today, have the courage to allow yourself to emerge and to act within your values.

September 13

Living boldly
By stepping
Into opportunity
That serves
Authentic living
And balance
By working to
Live by
Your own
Set of standards
Is
Fearless.

The world is filled with standards set by others. Some of these standards are below the level of decency, and some standards are so average, they mean nothing. When you set your own standards, you can make sure they are extraordinary.

Life is a work in progress, but don't wait to live your standards until they are perfect. Live your standards as a lesson in daily improvement. This is a fearless life.

In your daily meditation, reflect on your standards for living. Determine where your standards can be strengthened, and give yourself permission to live by your own standards, even if they are imperfect.

September 14

My circles run
The same pattern
Each day.
This is a
Great comfort
To my senses,
But I realize
My comfort
Blocks courage
To move into new
Circles
And to try
A new adventure.
I determine while
Fearing my lack
Of comfort
To break
Repeating patterns.

It is easy and comfortable to stick to our daily routines. To keep growing as a person, use your courage to take an adventure, do something new that will require you to tackle it with rigor.

To free your courage and start your adventure, think about those adventures you most want to try. You don't have to think about adventure as a physical activity; adventure can be anything you want. Learning to cook, taking a class, or even reading a difficult book can be an adventure.

Today, think about how you might break your current routine. Try a new adventure. Take the steps to put your adventure into action.

September 15

The rush of
Completing my list
Keeps my mind
In constant
Movement.
Fearing missing
A check on
The list,
With a breath,
Centering
my mind to be
Still,
I need courage
To be present
With myself
And to be guided
To live not
By a list
But by
My values.

In a rushed and hurried world, a person requires bravery to stop. It is important to take time to be completely still in both mind and body each day. Breathing and reconnecting to the core of who you are is important daily.

When our checklists and our tasks begin to be more important than our own values, we lose ourselves; we have so much fear about missing something that we actually miss the right stuff.

Today, put your list away for an hour and spend that time connecting to what you value in life. Review your list and determine how aligned you are to what you value. Cross off those tasks that are not aligned, breathe in your quiet moment, and have the courage to live beyond a list.

September 16

My hero
Lives a
Life of
Courageous
Imperfection.
She willingly
Opens to others,
Successfully
Changing her
Part of the
World because
She is not
Perfect
But
Authentic.

Waiting to live life until you get everything perfect wastes precious moments of living. It takes courage to put yourself out in the world to do meaningful work.

Putting yourself out into the world doesn't always work out perfectly, and that is okay. Imperfections are part of living. We can't let them block our way to meaningful work. If you are doing your best to be exceptional, then let the imperfections come forward as your lessons.

Determine if you are holding back from getting out into the world because you are waiting to be perfect. Find one way to put yourself out into the world in spite of not having everything perfect. Talk about your goals. Begin to share with small groups of people your dreams. Be authentic to yourself. Do not fear. Be courageous.

September 17

My heart feels

The words

My mouth is

Unable to form.

The words

Sit inside,

Waiting

For me

To face

Them and

Bravely

Speak

My version

Of the truth.

Speaking up for yourself or for others takes courage. We often feel we should speak what is in our hearts but miss the opportunity to say the words. We worry about causing more conflict because our words may offend or cause hurt.

Using our words to speak the truth needs to be weighed with living our purpose. Are the words designed to make a change or to allow healing? Our words may still cause conflict, but the words we chose and the way we reveal our truths is important. Our words reveal whether we use our words to heal or to hurt.

Today, think about what your heart feels should be spoken. Reflect on how the words will heal you or will help heal others. Begin to frame the words, and hear the words you need to say. Frame your words with healing.

September 18

She questions
Her purpose,
Her reason for
Being placed
In current
Places,
And I realize
The gift she
Provides to
My own
Life questions
That demand
A brave
Moment of
Uncertainty,
Checking my own
Path, place, purpose.

Taking time to periodically question the path you are on and the purpose of what you are doing is healthy. It takes some courage to thoroughly question your purpose, because the answers may not be what you want to hear.

Questioning various areas of life helps us to stop drifting through life and being stagnant rather than thriving. When we live fully engaged lives, the questioning never ends; we question where we are at and where we want to be at age eighteen and at age sixty.

Use today to take stock of your path, place, and purpose. Ask yourself if you are indeed thriving, making a difference, and feeling happiness. All of these are important questions throughout your life. Be brave enough to listen to the answers and act on them.

September 19

Questioning my self-worth
With those
Who question my
Place in their
World,
I strive to
Hide my
Lacking,
And then
I believe
In myself.
Bearing all
My courage,
I stand
And release
Those with questions
Pondering my lacking,
And I question
A world that
Makes any human
Feel less.

The courage to believe in yourself even when others don't is important to living a fully engaged life. It is important to never allow people who don't believe in you to have power over you or to make you feel less.

It may take a great deal of courage to stand up for yourself, but it takes even more courage to discount others' view of you and to believe in yourself. Questioning anyone who devalues others is an act of bravery.

Today, question those who are not inclusive in their actions and words. Stand for yourself and others by being inclusive in your actions and words. Start with one action that will demonstrate your value of a person or group that is not included in your current group of friends.

September 20

Persisting with
Questions
In spite of the strife
Caused,
I determine
To look
Directly at
Injustice
And with
Determination
Decide
I must persist
Asking, risking, doing.

The world is filled with injustice, and it can be easy to turn away rather than face it and question it. Living with courage goes beyond facing and questioning injustice, however. Courage is about persisting in acting to correct injustice.

When we make the decision to correct injustice, it becomes a lifelong cause that we willingly commit time, energy, and passion to daily; we will continue to bravely ask questions while being willing to risk ourselves for others and persist in doing more.

Reflect today on your own courage to persist in positively changing injustices. Today, make a plan to persist in questioning and acting on the injustice that you are willing face.

September 21

The attack

Lacks

Bravery while

Mean words

To hurt

A living

Spirit

Continue.

The courageous

Find

Paths

To teach.

They use words

Of healing

And do not allow

The counterattack

To have

Power.

It is never brave to use words to hurt another person. Eventually, these angry words and feelings come back to your own spirit.

When you feel you have been wronged, it takes immense courage to follow the path of healing. Following the path of healing benefits not only yourself but also those who have hurt you.

Reflect today on your choices to hurt or heal. Find the courage to resist attacking, and turn toward activity that heals you and those who have hurt you.

September 22

Thousands of
Images bombard
Me.
These
Women without
Curving bosom and bottom
Never quite
Fit my mirror.
The struggle to
Be myself
Is an
Accomplishment
As I refuse
To allow the
Bombardment
To control my
Own mirror.

Aging is a courageous journey, and throughout the journey, accepting and loving your own image is often difficult. We are surrounded with images that don't fit what we see in our own mirrors. It takes courage to work toward your own image without the influences of others.

All people have things they don't like about themselves. A healthy body image isn't about letting your body go without care but about working on those habits we can improve to maintain well-being.

Maintaining your well-being starts with defining what your well-being looks and feels like. Working to maintain your health is key. Then you can create your own image rather than try to conform to images that don't belong to your body.

September 23

Over a lifetime
There are
Changes
And I am
Transformed by
The daily events
Around me.
The laughter
The hardships
All have an impact
And leave a mark
But by the gritting
Of my teeth
I deny
Changes aimed at
Reducing the essence
Of who I am.

The events of our lives have an impact on us. The laughter and the hardships transform us daily, but we must guard against them changing the core of who we are.

It can be easy to fall into negative thinking after a disappointment or to allow a tragedy to take away our ability to live. All events leave their marks. Working to maintain the essence of ourselves is critical.

Consider those events that have left lasting marks on you. Reflect on the those marks and if those events have been allowed to change the core of you. Make efforts to find the you that you know and love.

September 24

There have been
People in my life
Wishing to define
Who I am
And my calling,
But I am
Not their
Victim
And I will
Never be bullied
Into accepting
Someone else's
Definition
Of my life,
For only I
Define me.

You alone define who you are and what you will be. There will always be people who want to put you into a category, but don't allow anyone to bully you away from being yourself.

It can be easy to allow someone else to relegate you to a category, whether wife, homemaker, or worker. If you see yourself as a writer, artist, or anything else, have the courage to define yourself that way.

Reflect on the categories that people put you in, and determine if those categories are accurate to you. Begin to think about defining yourself, and with no apology, make it so.

September 25

The two I

Watch

Rally through life

With triumphs

And challenges,

My job done,

And now

There is courage

To let them

Be just who they are

And to let them know

All is accepted.

There comes a time when you have provided the foundation and you need to give acceptance to allow those you love to be who they are. It takes courage to be true to the acceptance you give to others.

Acceptance isn't passive but active. It supports decisions with love and allows failure without judgment. Providing this support juggles stepping back and forward with support. It isn't easy or perfect.

Determine who needs your true acceptance. Find the steps that you can begin to take to actively let those you love know that you accept them as they are. Know that you won't be perfect but that you can courageously continue on the acceptance journey.

September 26

Be drawn
By the pull of
Your calling,
The work that
Brings you passion
To go beyond,
To make the world
Better.
Boldly embrace
This part of you
And you will
Model for others
Bravery.

We often find ourselves in places in life that we have settled into by accident. Thinking about our original goals as being from our past and unreachable is a habit to break.

Sometimes goals cannot be met in the way we had intended, but the passion that drew us to those goals can still be a part of our lives. It may be through volunteerism or in a smaller role, but you can work toward living your passion with courage.

Today, take time to reexamine your current life. Does it include your passion, and are you living your calling? Take steps to understand your passion and to move closer to engaging in it.

September 27

Compromising

Your

Values, beliefs, or dreams

Is a betrayal

With long-lasting

Scars,

But healing

Starts with

Picking

Your

Values, beliefs, and dreams

Up

And giving honor

To them

By opening

The world

To see

You living

Fully fearless

With each value,

Each belief,

And each dream.

Keeping true to your own values, beliefs, and dreams requires daily work. When we compromise the most important parts of who we are, we need to begin healing by starting over with a recommitment to our values, beliefs, and dreams.

Sometimes we do miss the mark with our values, beliefs, or dreams, and that leaves a mark on our spirits. Moving forward to get back on track is very important. Taking those steps to get on track is brave and honorable, and it helps build values, beliefs, and dreams.

Today, determine to honor your own values, beliefs, and dreams by living them. This means you put them out into the world and put them to work. When you have a day when things don't go the right way, make it right by acknowledging that and making a change.

September 28

It is rare
And beautiful
To be
The woman
Being
Unapologetically
Who she is,
Comfortable
With her past
And creating her future
With authentic
Imperfections.
This courageous life
Is the essence
Of beauty.

People who can be themselves throughout their daily lives with no apology have great courage in a world filled with plastic people. Those who can embrace their past and their imperfections have the best chance at living full and engaged lives.

There is great beauty in a woman who is uncomplicated in her acceptance of herself. Although it is difficult to accomplish, working at deep acceptance through a lifetime provides centered happiness.

Reflect on your own ability to accept who you are with no apology. If there are areas that are blocking your ability to create the best future you can have, work at releasing them.

September 29

Your unique
Life force
And energy
Express
Your daily art of
Living
Matched by
No one,
Because in the world,
There is only
One of you—
Exceptional
And valuable.
You need to
Fiercely protect
Yourself as
A rare and
Irreplaceable
Gift.

A person requires bravery to acknowledge the special uniqueness and life force within his or her spirit. It is important that your thoughts and actions honor your gifts and that you are aware of what makes you special.

The actions that each person needs to embrace every day are those that protect the unique energy that person brings to each day. Many people find it is easy to protect others, but bravery is required for a person to protect him or herself.

Today, take time to reflect on your own unique gifts. Determine how you are protecting your uniqueness. Call on your courage to live a life of valuing yourself.

September 30

With intention,

My journey

Is filled with

Those things

I fear

And those

I love.

My challenge

Is to embrace all

With the courage

To live

Outside of myself

And inside of myself

With continual hope

That one more day

Is a good one.

Perhaps the bravest of us all are those who remain hopeful and keep hope alive for others. Whether facing fear of something or a challenge that seems impossible, the hopeful have the tools to conquer what they face.

Real hope is difficult to maintain and requires continual balancing, nurturing, forgiving, and reflecting on what is important. Hopeful people are contagious and give others the courage to hope.

As you reflect on living with courage, also check your level of hope. If there is an area in your life that you are struggling with, decide to approach it with new hope. Find one person in need of hope today, and provide that person a picture of hope.

October

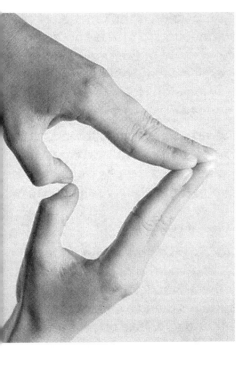

Compassion is a science and art that every person needs to practice each day. Practicing compassion is not a precise science because there are so many facets to it.

Compassion requires a deep awareness of yourself and of others. Knowing that our time on this earth is limited creates an urgency in us to reach out to others. A belief in each person's value adds depth to our awareness.

We are all connected to each other and to our planet. Realization of this interdependence takes away the arrogance that keeps us separated. This allows us to reach out to others without expectation. This month, build your practice of compassion.

October Focuses

Practice compassion.

Begin to be aware of others.

Connect to others.

October 1

Compassion
Lifelong practices
Of awareness
Of self and others
Focused
Bone-deep caring
Loving each living being
For the value
Each brings to
The world.

Compassion is the practice of connecting to others and being fully aware of their value. Although we all have the ability to act with compassion to some extent, we all need to practice it daily.

Compassion is the gift we give to others and our world. When we value others deeply, we make our world better, but we all have to be active and purposeful with this kind of compassion.

Today, take time to meditate on your own level of connecting to others. Practicing compassion requires being aware of the people around you. Take one hour today to concentrate on those around you.

October 2

Hear the words
As you listen to
The heartbeat,
And through
Compassion,
Connection
Is made,
And awareness
Of our commonality
In humanness.

Listening deeply to another person involves more than hearing her or his words. You must be present and aware enough to listen to the person's heartbeat.

Listening at this level focuses all of your senses on the person. You can soak in the person's feelings and connect to them without pity or judgment. Connecting as a human to another human adds to our understanding of our commonness and moves us toward giving hope.

Listen with intent to someone today. Allow all of your senses to be part of the listening. Avoid thinking about your next comment or how you can fix the situation. With your touch, let the person know that you understand.

October 3

Every faith

Teaches

Love, compassion, and forgiveness

As powerful

Practices

Every person

Embeds into

Daily living

In order

To develop

Into a

Person

Of character.

It is no mistake that all of the world's religions focus on love, compassion, and forgiveness as the practices that every person should be involved in daily. People of character practice these daily, but not perfectly.

There are always areas for improvement, and there is not an expectation of perfection but an expectation of persistence in practicing every day.

Examine your own practice of love, compassion, and forgiveness. Determine your own places of improvement and develop a plan for this week to improve your practice.

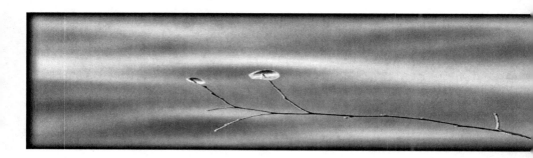

October 4

The garden
Of grief
Cultivates compassion
If your heart
Opens to pain
And allows
The opportunity
In life's
Search for
Connections
To others.

Everyone grieves or has experienced grief. After we have felt intense sorrow, we are most able to understand another person's pain. This kind of pain is part of life's journey, and we cannot avoid it, but it does provide benefit to us.

Grief cultivates compassion for others and connects us to others. Although grief causes us to hurt, cultivating compassion as a result of grief is positive. Being able to connect to others' suffering makes you a better person.

Today, think about the times you have been in grief. Reflect on using your grief to create a positive difference in yourself by cultivating your own compassion. Today, make a connection with someone you think is hurting, and use your compassion to connect to that person. Listen and lend a hand.

October 5

We are
Connected and
Interdependent
With all living beings
And our earth.
With deliberate
Awareness
Of being a part
Of a whole,
We can care
With a new level
Of involvement in
Living.

You cannot practice compassion without understanding your connections and interdependence on all life and your environment. We work hard to be independent for most of our lives, but in truth, understanding our interdependence develops our ability to care for others.

Caregivers often have the most difficult time allowing themselves to accept connection and interdependency, but when they do accept these things, their caring is brought to a new level. Caring for others and allowing others to care for you is practicing deliberate awareness of being part of a whole community.

Consider how you are connected with and live with interdependence in your life. Work today to strengthen your awareness of all beings in the corner of earth you walk. Connect through all your senses and reach out to tell one person about your connection to her or him and how you value that interdependence.

October 6

Begin with awareness

Of compassion

Filling in the

Cracks of

Your own soul

Recognizing you

Are rare and precious

With limited time

To actively engage

In compassion,

As pain

Is present daily

And compassion

Must overflow

Into the world

Around you.

To be fully compassionate to others, you have to have compassion for yourself. Being aware that you are worthy of being surrounded with compassion is important to you being able to send compassion out to others.

Recognizing that you are a rare and precious person allows you to better recognize this about all other beings. Everyone experiences pain, and being present with your own and others' pain is part of being compassionate.

Today, provide care to yourself and actively engage in being present within yourself. Don't be afraid of what is hurting you. Today, sit with what is hurting you, and turn it to a path of healing. This will allow you to send compassion into the world around you.

October 7

A new process in motion

Your body breathing

Deep in healing

Thoughts.

Provide spiritual

Inspiration

Moving down

Into each

Finger and toe.

Soaking into

Every part

Providing a

Force of life

That engages

In feeling deeply

For others.

Compassion that restores others begins with restoring yourself. Restoring yourself is having days in your life that quench your spirit's thirst and allow for time to inspire yourself by being in touch with your own feelings and surroundings.

Those days are vitally important to being present with others, for if you struggle with being present with yourself, you will struggle with being present with others.

For busy people, being present can be difficult but even more necessary for people with lives filled with activity. A full day of replenishing is a wonderful gift, but if the choice to replenish is an hour, make it count. You may find replenishment in the garden or in evening stargazing, but you need to find that time for being present with yourself. Today, find your hour to be present with yourself and schedule a day to restore yourself.

October 8

When we believe

Each person

Is rare and

Unique

We know

That person's footsteps

Cannot be

Walked in

And that

We may not

Need to understand

So much as

Listen

And feel

That story

As unique and

Rare.

One of the most important things we can do for the people who cross our paths is to turn toward them and pay attention to them. We have that choice every time someone turns toward us.

We may not understand that person's story, for every set of footprints takes a different path, but we can listen deliberately and with focus. Only when we listen at this level are we able to feel the story in front of us.

As people cross your path today, turn and pay attention to them with intentional and deliberate listening. Stop the internal conversations and focus yourself on the person honoring you with his or her story. Remember that the person in front of you is unrepeatable, as is that person's story.

October 9

Participate in creating
The world
With acts of
Compassion
Toward
All beings.
The patch
Of earth
We stand on
Must be
At the forefront of
Every moment and
Each breathe
To make a difference.

Every day, we have the privilege and opportunity to participate in creating a better world. Some may think one person cannot make the world better, but each time we are kind to a person or kind to the earth, we create a ripple that is sent out to places we don't even know.

Participating in making the world better can begin with a smile to a stranger or a check-in with a friend. You never know how kindness can change a person's day or even a person's life. The most important part of ceating a better world is using your opportunities to be kind.

Take time to believe that you do make a difference and that the things you do for other people make a ripple in the world. Participate in living with kindness today, and write down how you started a ripple today.

October 10

Unplugged

From your

Own life race

Be present

And fully attentive

To the movements

Of a face

And body

Belonging to the

One in front of

You

The connection

Allows feeling

Another's fleeting

Emotion

Enough to reach inside

And touch it.

To experience and practice compassion, you have to take time to disengage from your own fast-paced life and to be fully present with those who come to you. When you are able to put aside your own to-do list for a moment, you have the opportunity to engage in compassion.

Being present with someone is a gift to both of you. It requires listening to the words coming from the other person and seeing the body in front of you expressing the feelings we so often miss. It is important to stay focused on the one in front of you. Hearing and feeling in this manner engages your own body and internal senses.

Make a conscience effort to unplug from your own worries and needs today in order to connect to another person. Be attentive to that person's words and feelings, and respond to his or her needs. Determine what gifts you receive from being present for this other person.

October 11

Morning unfolds
And with a stretch
I begin
A new
Experience
Of venturing
Into a world
Filled with people
Who need
My smile
So in the
Morning light
I fill my own
Smile with
A deep belly breath
And an awareness
Of myself.

One practice of compassion is to begin each day by centering yourself. Start each day by filling your smile with reminders of what compassion is and how to train your thoughts and actions to live the day with compassion.

When you decide you will provide for others, you must start by ensuring that you have positive energy flowing through yourself. This energy flow can start with the first morning stretch and end with calm evening breathing.

Take care that you are aware of yourself, and repeat to yourself that you are also worthy of compassion; this fills your spirit. Today, take your own awareness seriously and examine your energy flow. Provide yourself reminders of your worthiness.

October 12

The big things
In life
Matter.
The rest is fleeting
And will not matter
In two weeks
In ten years
Over a lifetime.
But in the moment
The focus
Of little things
Can affect a thousand
Circles in the pool
And drown compassion
By the noise of
Each circle.

We often focus on the many little things that don't matter in the broader view of happiness. When we focus on those things, they often have a ripple effect and move the negative forward.

If we can put the little irritations of the day in perspective while they are occurring, we can begin the practice of compassion. Working to keep your focus on the important and positive in your world makes a difference in what you are putting out into the world.

Reflect on what you are focused on during the day. Determine if you are focused on important and meaningful ideas, and assess what ripples you are sending out into your family and environment. Let the irritations fall away, and move toward those ideas that ripple in positive ways.

October 13

Providing compassionate hope

Requires rigor

With discipline

And high standards

Of living,

Inspiring with

Real dialogue,

And challenging

To rise above

Challenges,

Done with

Love, faith and hope.

Living with compassion is not possible without using the discipline of high standards of living and having rigorous expectations for ourselves and others. Compassion that provides hope must be accompanied by challenging and truthful dialogue.

Compassion is not the same as giving in to people not meeting their potential. With love, faith, and hope, compassion lifts others to move beyond life's obstacles and meet their potentials.

Today, reflect on your ability to lift others with disciplined compassion. When real and truthful dialogue is needed, make sure you are able to provide this with love, faith, and hope.

October 14

Anger
Clouds
My internal
Practice
Of giving
Care.
Knowing
Betrayal
Traps my
Compassion.
Lost,
I find
It is my
Own spirit
That is
Betrayed.

Living with anger is easy, but in the end, it betrays your spirit by blocking positive thinking. Anger is a powerful emotion that needs to be acknowledged and then turned toward the path of the positive actions of compassion.

Acknowledging your anger is the first step to removing the cloudy thinking it brings. It is important to determine if the source of the anger is important to address or, in the big picture, does not have meaning for you.

Moving anger to a path of positive thinking and action is important to your practice of compassion. Consider how you are dealing with your anger and turning it toward a positive path. List those things you are currently angry about, and determine if those things need attention or release. Think about how you might turn the anger toward the practice of compassion.

October 15

No expert

At living

In balance

And honoring

All beings

Within and outside

Of my own values,

I write

To remind myself

Of the heartbeats

Shared with me

And my connection

To each beat,

Becoming not

The expert

But another

Practitioner.

It is a daily practice to live in balance and compassion. There are no experts, only people working at it. None of us are able to do it perfectly but practice it daily.

When we realize that we are practitioners, we begin to understand that this is a journey of continuous learning rather than a task to get done. Improving our work in compassion is work that must be done day by day.

Reflect on your ability to work as a practitioner rather than as a perfectionist. Begin each day with a focus on practicing compassion and balance. When it doesn't work quite right, refocus and practice again.

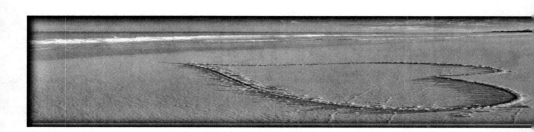

October 16

Creating

An environment

So others

Are centered

In peace

And find internal

Smiles

Requires, each day,

Involving

A slice of

Care.

This practice

In turn

Creates

Centering

Peace and

Your own

Internal

Happiness.

When we are able to create an environment that inspires others to be centered, we are able to center ourselves. Working daily to help others is what creates stable internal happiness.

Your internal smile starts your involvement in creating a world that is better for those you love and those you still haven't met. This kind of happiness is lasting.

Determine the environment you are creating for yourself and others. Find concrete examples of your activities that involve bettering your part of the world and creating centered happiness. Today, do one thing that centers your happiness.

October 17

There are

No words,

So none

Are formed.

It is with

Hands

Willing to reach

and touch,

It is with

Hearing and

Listening to another

Without my own

Internal voice chattering,

And it is with

A heart

Connecting to

Feelings

That must be felt

Together

That I

Exercise

Compassion.

Having the right words is not as important as being willing to engage with and to reach out to one in need. Compassion is being present by actively listening without working to prepare a response, and connecting to the feelings being shared with you.

Reaching out with a touch when it is needed can be more powerful than words. The silence of just being there can be powerfully healing. Healing only takes a willingness to reach out to another person.

Reach out today without pre-forming words. Allow yourself to touch, listen, and feel with a person in need. With courage, meet that person where he or she is, and work your compassion.

October 18

Two lizards
Sharing
Garden space
Greet me
Each morning.
We work quietly
Together.
Connecting
Our work
Allows me
To see
Small beings
And feel a part of
Their cycle
Of the day.

The world around us offers many opportunities to demonstrate and find compassion. You will find such opportunities right in your own backyard. Sharing space with and becoming aware of the living beings and plants around you can provide great comfort and peace.

Awareness of these beings is the first step and requires us to be still and present with ourselves and our surroundings. The quiet in your mind and spirit will ready you for full awareness.

Step outside today and still yourself. Make note of what comes to all your senses. Feel connections to the earth and the small and large sharing your earth space. Do this daily to grow compassion.

October 19

She worries
That her heart
Doesn't feel
Like others,
That something
May be wrong.
But her heart
Has beaten inside of mine
And I know her journey
Of intense feelings.
She will
Face them.
Her outpouring
Will change
Others,
And she will
Feel
Her own kindness
Surround
Her own heart.

There are times when we may worry that we don't feel compassion like everyone else. The wonderful thing about practicing compassion is that it looks different for every person. There is no step-by-step manual for practicing compassion.

Compassion flows through us in different ways and affects people, places, and situations differently. This is a good thing, because people, places, and situations can draw strength from many people and take something new from each. Practicing compassion requires that we have an awareness of others and then are willing to make contact.

In the next few days, know that if you are aware of other people, of this earth, of situations, and are willing to connect with them to make things better, you are practicing compassion. Reflect on how you connect, and be willing to strengthen your connections.

October 20

In his hands
Is an instant
Understanding
Of safeness
And complete acceptance
Teaching me
How important
Touch is
To connecting
Beyond words.
He reaches
To cover my hand
But holds my heart.

We have people in our life who have provided us care, understanding, and unlimited kindness. Those people are the teachers of compassion. We are lucky when they come into our lives, even if they only pass through on their own journeys.

Those practitioners have lessons to teach us. They can be famous teachers leaving lessons for thought, or they can be seemingly normal people in our lives. These are people we need to aware of and learn from, and we need to apply compassion like they do.

Find your teachers of compassion. Watch and learn from them. Today, let them know you are learning from them, and give them gratitude for their teachings of compassion.

October 21

A sense of

Peacefulness

And belonging

Fills my heart

Each time

I am reminded

Of my connection

To those

Who are invited

To share

My sacred

Place called home.

Without the connection

To others

My potential

Is lessened.

Connection to others is essential to developing strong compassion. Understanding that we are connected and have an interdependence with other people can bring the human lens into focus.

We often want to be independent and may hesitate to get involved with people and connect to their lives and hearts. Connection does takes time and it does get messy, but it also provides you the chance to use the gift of your compassion.

Today, think about your connections with others. Reconnect with someone you miss, or make a call to someone you feel may need a connection.

October 22

A heart must be
Exercised
With daily
Extension of
Rigorous beating
By reaching for
Others,
Lifting those
Around you
And carrying
One unable to
Walk today.
This lengthens the
Life of every
Heart.

Practicing compassion is a daily exercise to keep you balanced and healthy. Being aware of others in need and being willing to lift them and even carry them is the practice of compassion.

While you help others, practicing compassion also helps you. It creates a more centered and balanced person. It places a smile inside, and this helps your own heart.

Today, be determined to practice compassion with another person. Take time to see how compassion affects your body and how it makes you feel. Keep practicing and feel your benefits.

October 23

You may never pay back
Those
Who sustained you
In moments
Of need.
Human generosity
Inspires
An appreciation,
Allowing
Not only gratitude
But also the willingness
To generate
Compassion forward
To the next
Moment of
Need.

There have been people in your life who have sustained you during difficult times. The help they provided made a difference in your life, and there are no words of thanks that can match their actions.

But their help can inspire you to willingly generate compassion forward to a person in need who crosses your path. Having models of people who give with no expectation of receiving is helpful, but you can pass forward care even without those models.

Think about those who have provided for you when you were in need. Let their actions inspire you to help someone at work or at home. Remember, there are no words for repayment; just remind them to pay it forward when they are able.

October 24

Those in hardship

Are sending out

Letters

Of need,

Simple requests

For connection

Affirming

For them that

They are rare

And precious

Beings

Worthy of

A human hand.

Respond

To their letters

By turning

Toward them

And holding

Their hands

Until they are

Warmed

And able to

Hold another's hand.

At different times, both people we know and people we don't know need our connection. It is important that we respond to those in need of connection.

Such a response may be a touch, a smile, or being present in a moment of need. Making sure that we let people needing connection know that they are worthy of the connection.

Search your family and community to find those people needing connection to others. Reach out and provide them with those needing connections.

October 25

Petals opening
Individually,
Growing in mud,
Beauty, and wisdom,
Moving above the mud,
But roots
Grounded
In shared
Mud.
You cannot
Avoid the mud
If you plan to grow
Wisdom and beauty
And allow your own petals
To open.

Compassion is messy, and it demands a willingness to get in and participate in the work. That means that we sometimes need to be knee-deep in the mud. But the earth's rich dirt also allows us to help others grow and enriches our own lives.

Never be afraid to engage in life's messy parts, because they offer an opportunity for learning and can create both beauty and wisdom in your life. This kind of compassion also keeps you grounded.

Reflect on your willingness to engage in the messy parts of life. Whether your messy parts of life are in a relationship, in the community, or in yourself, be willing to dig in and engage in practicing your compassion. The messy parts of living are also the ones that can ground you for growth.

October 26

The greatest
Kindness
Is to love
Without needing
Change.
It is my greatest
Gift to
Participate
In experiences
Revealing
To others and myself
The possibility
Of change.

Accepting another person is a great kindness. While having no expectation for change, it is also a gift when you authentically participate in experiences that reveal to others the possibility of change.

Balancing, accepting, and challenging those you love is difficult. It is not about determining the changes needed for someone else but participating in experiences that reveal their new potential.

Today, think about the kindness you give in acceptance and the gift of challenge you extend to those people who are important to you.

October 27

Daily rituals of
Work and family
Do not create
A life of living.
It is when
You have
Reached out
And touched someone
With care
By doing something
With no expectation
Of return
Or repayment
That you create
A life
Lived.

It is easy to stay within the comfort of daily rituals. Practitioners of compassion live to reach outside of their daily routine, and make a difference for other people.

We often have pictures of making differences that are life-changing, but making a difference can be as simple as taking time to be present with another person even for just a moment. Life-changing differences are fabulous, but a quiet smile that lifts a spirit is priceless.

Today, take time to lift another spirit by doing something with no expectation of thanks. You choose to do something anonymously. Move out of your comfort zone to make a difference.

October 28

In this journey
Of life
Beginning for all at
Different times
And places
There is a miracle
Of intersection
Where shared
Kindness, love, and compassion
Inspire
Hopefulness
And lift
The journey
Even when the
Miracle of intersection
Lasts only a
Moment.

We often affect people and are not even aware of it. Such an effect can happen with a word, a smile, or an action, and it takes only a moment when paths cross. We have a great opportunity every day to pass through and have a positive effect on others' lives.

The choice to use our time and energy in positive or negative activities is present daily. We can choose to smile at a person and give positive energy or to turn away from a person. Both actions make an impact.

To practice compassion is to use the moments of intersecting with others to create a positive effect. Today, be determined to cross paths with people using your positive energy.

October 29

When you are viewed

As a "They"

Or "One of Those"

By good people

There is a

Lesson of compassion

That helps you

Develop heart

To help those

Separated

And you are

Able to feel

Their need

To be

An

Us.

The experience of being on the outside is a lesson in developing compassion for others who are also on the outside. The experience of being "one of them" makes you realize the importance of inclusion.

It is our differences that make us stronger as a unit of humanity. To include others is to reach out with understanding and open the opportunity to learn.

Today, reach out to someone you have viewed as separate from your current group. Determine to learn from this person and provide for her or him the gift of inclusion.

October 30

Believing that your own
One true path
Is right for all
Binds you
To rigid and
Narrow judgments.
This arrogance will
Limit the rich
Intersections
Through other paths
That provide
Knowledge and
Understanding
Of all humanity.

There are many paths to take to be a productive and caring part of the human family. When we become so rigid that we believe there is only one path for all, we become arrogant and unable to practice compassion.

This doesn't mean you should abandon your own path or that your path should not be honored. What it does mean is that you have to allow for others to follow their own paths and encourage yourself to intersect with others to allow your own understanding to increase.

In a still moment, release your judgments of others and move toward acceptance of the paths chosen by others. Be open to seeking others who are not on your path, and work to increase your own understanding and compassion.

October 31

The nature of compassion
Acts on knowledge
That suffering happens daily.
It isn't about ending
All suffering but
Doing what you can
Without acknowledgment
Because you know
Giving
Compassion
To one
Is the right
Path
To take.

Compassion is not about just feeling or listening to hurt but also being willing to take action. It is a willingness to commit to involvement.

Although listening deeply is a wonderful quality, the willingness to be engaged in the mud and to get our hands in the mix can be frightening. It is the essence of living in compassion.

In the month of October, you have focused on living with compassion. Decide what you are willing to be involved with at an intimate level. Today, take action to be involved and use your skills of compassion to make a difference.

November

Embracing a life filled with gratitude is November's focus. Gratitude is connected with joy, as the cycle of gratitude and joy is increased each time we engage in being grateful. Part of being grateful is giving to those in need. Those who live lives of gratitude always have something to give back to those in need.

We sometimes make our lives complicated, but living a life of gratitude is simple. It requires only taking time to say "thank you" for what is in front of you and what is around you each day. Those thoughtful moments of thanks can generate daily joy.

November Focuses

Gratitude is connected with joy.

Gratitude can be shown with a simple thank-you.

Gratitude gives back.

November 1

Gratitude
Bows my head
And fills
My heart
Daily
In order
To engage
In acts of
Gratefulness
And open
My eyes
To the small miracles
Walking
Through
My path.

Gratitude is both an attitude and an activity that needs to be completed each day. On each day that we engage in true thanks, our eyes open to our daily miracles. The way we participate in gratitude is different for every person, but it is important to find the way that works for you.

Knowing that gratitude serves to provide you with a level of happiness that centers and balances you is reason enough to be grateful for all you have and fills your heart with positive feelings that last through the day.

Today, bow your head or take a moment to give silent thanks. Become aware of how giving thanks makes you feel. Be thankful for your daily miracles.

November 2

Walk with feet
Willing to
Touch the earth
With reverence,
Softly engaging
In experiencing
The amazing
Patch of earth
Underfoot.
I am
Thankful
My feet
Take a moment
To completely join
With where
I stand.

Each morning that we touch our earth, we need to have reverence and thankfulness for what the earth provides for us every day. As you walk through the day, it is important to be aware of the gifts provided by the patch of earth you call home.

To be able to join with the earth is to be willing to stop the daily rush, become aware, and connect with the earth. In that moment, feeling the breeze in your face, the sun's warmth, or the grass under your feet is your focus.

Every day, take at least one moment to enjoy your surroundings. Give thanks for the world around you. Find beauty in your own backyard.

November 3

Life is filled
With daily
Struggles,
Some knocking
Your breath from
Your body.
But fight to breathe
Through thankfulness,
Understanding that
A happy life
Is not void of
Struggle.
A happy
Life
Is the ability
To deal with
Struggle
And breathe.

Don't wait to be grateful until everything is perfect or in place. Life is filled with struggle for everyone regularly. It is not the lack of struggle that allows us to be happy, but the ability to cope with struggle.

We often think we need things to be good for us to feel grateful. A different way of thinking of gratitude is to be thankful for the struggles, because they are our teachers. We also want to be thankful for our own ability to deal with the struggles that come our way.

With a deep breath, give thanks for your struggles and frame your struggles as your teachers. Be confident in your ability to meet your struggles head-on and to deal with them.

November 4

The mistake

Is not the

Focus.

It is

What you

Are able to

Do with the

Mistake that

Matters.

Not a retreat

But a willingness

To sing again

With a thankful

Heart for

The mistakes

That have made you

Better.

Mistakes are part of each person's past and future. A mistake can be painful to move through, but you can step through your mistakes. You do this by focusing not on the mistake but on what you do after the mistake.

It is important to take responsibility for what you have done and take whatever consequences come with the mistake. After that, it is important to learn from the mistake and do something with your learning.

We all need to be thankful for those mistakes that have made us better people. Think about a mistake you made and what you need to do to learn from it and make a difference with others.

November 5

Gratitude is simple
With no need
For drama,
Filled
With gifts and talents
Needed to
Fulfill our
Intended purpose,
And with simplicity
We give
Thanks
For the blessings
Our gifts
Bring.

Do not make being grateful complicated. It is simple. When we stop long enough to recognize that we have been provided with many gifts and talents to help us achieve our potential, we can experience a moment of thanks.

Recognizing your gifts and talents is part of the process of doing the things that make you happy and others better. In the process of doing, we find our purpose.

Each day, with simplicity, give thanks for the blessings you have and the ability to help others by using the gifts given to you. Whether you offer it in a silent thank-you or a song of thanks, make sure you express your gratitude.

November 6

Gratitude

Turns

What we have

To what

Is needed.

A thankful heart

Turns denial

Into acceptance

And gives clarity

To our

Past,

Opening us to

A peaceful

Present

And possibility

For the future.

When you practice gratitude, you view the things in your life through a different lens. The change in focus allows you to see beyond you what you have to what you need and to your ability to give to another.

Gratitude, which fills us with acceptance and peace about what we do have in life, provides us with hope. Filling our hearts with thankfulness gives us clarity about our own situations.

Today, with eyes closed, picture your own heart being filled with gratitude for those things you do have. We all have holes and needs, but focus today on what you do have—count fingers, toes, and smiles.

November 7

In morning light
I am thankful
For the new day
And that I have
A harbor for
Resting and renewing.
I am aware of
My blessings
As I am able
To work, laugh, and play,
And I am
Grateful
For grace and goodness
In my life.

The morning's first light provides a special time for giving thanks. Wherever your current harbor is, give thanks for it. It is providing needed rest and rejuvenation.

Take time to be aware of the many blessings surrounding you. No matter where you are, there are blessings to become attuned to each day—even if it is only the change in the season tapping your window.

Work this morning at soaking in the many miracles around your harbor. Use each of your senses to become fully aware of the things that benefit you. Take time to be grateful, and repeat this practice each morning.

November 8

His eyes seek

Mine and

I am

Immediately

Aware of

Heartfelt

Gratitude,

Waiting

A lifetime

For him

To provide

Connection to

My past and future,

Blessing me

With happiness

Each time

Our eyes meet

And we smile.

There are probably people in your life who have the ability to fill your heart with gratitude. It only takes your eyes meeting to cause you to feel that you have much to be grateful for in your life.

When you have connections in your life, you are a fortunate. It is important to nurture the connections you have and to find time to give thanks for those connections.

Today, tell those people who make a difference in your life that you are grateful for them being in your life. Make a plan to strengthen the connections that you are grateful for each day.

November 9

A walk on water

Is not the

Everyday

Miracle,

But our

Miracles are

Present

As we walk

Each day

On the green

Earth.

Seeing

The ants

Working together

To carry an

Enormous weight

Allows us

To be present in

A miracle and

Feel alive.

There are miracles around us every day, and it takes only a moment to recognize the miracles happening in your path. Taking time to be thankful for the small and large miracles you encounter each day is essential to being happy.

Being open to seeing miracles may be the first step. The many amazing things we see daily in our own backyards are part of the many miracles we can witness. Miracles are there in the form of bees pollinating, a spider's web, or ants that take care of each other by working together.

Open yourself to your own daily miracles, and be thankful they have crossed your path today. Search every day for miracles to fill you with joy and gratitude.

November 10

Desert dwellers
Wait for
Wet drops of
Rain to
Soak
Their
Dry and
Upturned
Palms
In
Gratitude
The water
Fills
A soul.

Rain in any desert is a gift. It supplies a new way of looking at the world and provides nourishment for all those wishing for continued growth. There are rainmakers in our world who deserve our gratitude.

For those who provide a new way of looking at the world—the artists, writers, and thinkers—we give thanks. For those who provide nourishment for continued growth—the parents, teachers, and healers of body and spirit—we give thanks.

Without delay, reach out to your rainmakers and replenish their gifts. Be specific in your thank-you to them, and let them know they have made a difference in your life.

November 11

Lucky me

For there

Are people

Only needing to

Walk into

My room

And

Their smiles

Infectiously

Fill me with

Grounded

Happiness

Transforming

My soul

Into a grateful

Being

We are sometimes surprised that the little things we do make a difference to someone else. Such a little thing may be coming in to work and making sure you ask another person how she is, and really listening to her.

You have people in your life who make a difference who may not know the difference they are making in your life. Becoming aware of how your own actions and the actions of others positively affect those who pass through your day is part of practicing deliberate gratitude.

Find those people who have made a difference in your life and let them know of the difference they made in your life. Today make a difference for others by really working today at being aware of eye contact, smiles, and daily actions of yourself and those around you. Let those connecting with you know they have made a difference.

November 12

Living once,

A span

Of only

Moments,

Without sadness

Of ending,

I feel

Deep gratitude

For my

Own moments.

Silently, I vow

To cherish

My time.

It is important that we understand how limited our moments are in this lifetime. Understanding the limits on our time brings each day into focus and helps us be grateful for every day we have.

It is critical that, without sadness, we give thanks for every day we have and make the most of all the talents we have. Our gratitude is deepened when we use our time to lift others.

Take a silent vow to cherish your days and to daily make the most of the gifts you provide to others. Allow your gratitude to fill yourself and others.

November 13

Grateful for
The strength
She instilled,
The fight
To stand for
Myself,
The ability
To be
Resilient
And move
Forward
In spite
Of mistakes.
For this
I am
Grateful.
She was
My mother.

Being a parent is difficult, and no one gets it perfect, but your parents provided you with a unique perspective. Although your life has been influenced by your parents and family, you have the ability and responsibility to direct your own path. A positive path includes giving thanks to those who gave you the strength to find your own path.

It is good to let those who have had an impact on your life to know this while they are alive and well. Sharing this information freely is a gift, especially to your parents, who know they made mistakes but did their best.

Reflect on those who gave you strength to be who you are today. If they are still here, let them know. If they are gone, offer a silent message of thanks, as they are always with you.

November 14

Telling others
About
Our blessings
Is not a
Measure
Of thankfulness
Or a way of living
Authentic gratitude.
Using our blessings
To better the world
Speaks
To dwelling in grace.

We have much to be grateful for each day. We can be thankful for those things in our lives, but the biggest measure of our thankfulness is how we use our blessings to make better our own part of the world.

Living authentic gratitude is an active process. It engages us in using our talents and resources to lift others and to encourage others to use their gifts to lift those they come in contact with.

Give silent thanks for your talents and resources that make you better. Decide how you might use those resources to help someone you know.

November 15

Simple
And forward
Words
Communicating
All needed
Heartfelt
Thank-yous
Each day
Provide
Needed
Gratitude
In living life.

It is uncomplicated, the practice of gratitude. The simplicity of giving a daily thank-you for your gifts and talents begins with the words "thank you." Providing a thank-you to those giving gifts and talents to you is awe-inspiring.

The words "thank you" can create a difference in a day and in a life when given from the heart. Taking time to feel the words as you say them strengthens your connections with others, with nature, and with yourself.

Today, start a practice of giving gratitude by incorporating the simple words "thank you"—not by just saying them, but by feeling gratefulness so you mean them.

November 16

My morning prayer

Begins with

Gratefulness

For another

Morning stretch

And the family

Reaching out to me.

A walk to watering

My small

Patch of earth's green

Includes a smiling

Blessing for desert rain.

My only prayer

needed

Is "thank you."

The morning prayer starting your day begins not with asking for things but with listing those things in your present and past that make your life better. Those things making your life better are worth giving thanks for daily.

From your first morning stretch to the small and large tasks you are able to do each day, giving thanks each morning will start your day with positive energy. Giving thanks prior to asking for things also helps you focus on real needs.

Starting today, take time for morning thanks giving to frame your day on all that you do have. It all starts with the words "thank you."

November 17

Gratitude
Felt through
Hands and toes
Gently connects
Us to the wider
World of
Nature insisting
To us
That we
Are ingrained
In the broad
Web of
Energy and life
Surging
Through and
Around us.

The sense of belonging and connection moving through our lives can provide happiness. Our connection to nature lets us see that we are part of a bigger picture and part of the world's energy.

Being aware of this kind of connection to everything around you can bring a new level of energy to you, and a new level of comfort. It is for this sense of balance that we give gratitude.

Reflect on your own web of energy and connection to life. Be grateful for your connections, and allow the gratitude to fill you right down to your toes.

November 18

Practicing gratitude

And an ongoing

Sense of

Gratefulness

Not for the

Things we have

But for

The living gifts

Given to us,

We begin

To understand

Our own

Existence

As the

Supreme gift

To use

To better the world.

It is important that our practice of gratitude gives thankfulness for the things we have in our lives. The living gifts and the very life you have are the perfect place to start your gratitude practice.

When we are able to be authentically grateful for our own lives, we will be able to demonstrate, for all living beings on this earth, gratitude. This kind of gratefulness creates an environment that makes the world better.

With a breath, give thanks for your life and for all living beings. With this kind of gratitude, begin to use your own living gifts to do one thing today that makes a difference to a person you know and one thing that makes a difference to one person you don't know, or something for your patch of earth.

November 19

Powerful
Yet unassuming,
Gratitude
Is one
Of our
Greatest
Healers.
Invited into
Our hearts,
It allows us
To breathe in
Healing air
And to exhale
With
Life renewed.

Becoming a practitioner of gratitude has an unseen but felt benefit. Deeply felt gratitude has the power to heal your heart and spirit. Healing to your heart and spirit gives you a renewed life.

The key to active healing is fully recognizing what in your life is good and what you are thankful for daily. The next step to active healing is acting on your center of gratefulness, to reach out and help another person, cause, or community.

Breathe in the healing air of gratitude, and as you exhale, renew lives around you with your commitment to acting on your gratitude. Begin to acknowledge and sense your own heart and spirit healing.

November 20

Every language

In spoken

And unspoken

Tongue

Is full of words

Connecting us

With understanding

Communicated

With our eyes and hands.

The words

Are always

Understood:

Thank you.

Gracias

Ahéhee'

It is no mistake that all languages include words for expressing thanks. The power of these words must be taught to all and ingrained into our behaviors.

When gratitude is embedded as a part of who you are, acting to make sure that others benefit is easy. Those who model gratitude for their families, neighbors, and coworkers are the best teachers; they provide the lens to see the positive in both the large and small.

Today, be a model for gratitude. Teach your family, friends, and coworkers by your actions, and you will provide them the lens of gratitude.

November 21

All life-forms
Matter
And provide gifts
To the world.
We may not
Understand this
Until we
Gather in our
Own hearts
And see our
Existence as
A gift
And work
To serve
Our fellow
Forms of
Life.

Being able to see your own life as a gift to be treasured opens a new lens through which to view all life. When we view existence as a gift, we are able to see the value brought by all and to give thanks for our connections.

Daily recognition of the gift of living starts with an awareness that all we need is around us daily. Being thankful for what we have is the second part of this awareness. The awareness is as simple as feeling water quench your thirst and feeling the fall breeze on your face.

Take a moment right now to center yourself and to enjoy through all your senses what is around you. Be thankful for your own living, and begin to feel gratitude toward what and who are around you.

November 22

Joy and gratitude

Are linked closely,

For one of the

Ways to

Develop our

Ability to

Live in

Gratitude

Is to

Expand our

Daily joy

Of things

Small and large

In our own

Backyard.

Grateful people are also joyful people. Gratitude and joy are closely linked, as one affects the other. The more we are grateful, the more joy in our lives, and the more joy we find in our lives, the more we have to be grateful for every day.

Expanding the level of joy in your daily living builds your capacity for gratitude. It is like building up a savings account for those days when you need to be reminded of joy and gratitude.

Today, determine to bring some joy into your life and build your capacity to be grateful. Work at both joyfulness and gratefulness. Spend time reflecting on how building your capacity for living in gratitude works for you.

November 23

During our lives
Happiness
Ebbs and flows.
Experiences
Of joyfulness
Embed a physical
Imprint in our
Minds and bodies,
Allowing us
To find
Happiness
Again, and
For this
Ability to be
Imprinted again
With joy,
We give
Thanks.

We don't feel happy continually, but pleasant experiences are imprinted on our minds and bodies. Gratitude allows us to retrace those feelings to more easily experience them.

When we imprint joyful experiences, we are aware of how those experiences make us feel. The awareness of simple joy will provide the track for us to reexperience those feelings. Accepting that happiness and joy are not constant but that we can tap into these feelings by becoming aware of the times when we do feel joy is awesome.

Think back to the last time you felt grateful for your joy and happiness. Tap into how you felt with each of your senses. Use this memory to increase your ability to feel joyful. The more you experience the feeling, the easier joyfulness is to find during hard times.

November 24

With ease

I am able

To retrace

My joy journey

Because

It is a

Journey taken

Many times,

Allowing my

Mind, body, and spirit

To recognize

With gratitude

The cues

Of joy.

Recognizing joy throughout your entire mind, body, and spirit should be met not with indifference but with great gratitude that you feel joy.

Although joy ebbs and flows through our days and our lives, we need to recognize it when it is with us. Celebrating our ability to enjoy the journey allows us to work through the times that are not enjoyable.

Reflect on your journeys of joy. Determine how you are celebrating those moments. Find a quiet moment to be grateful for your joyful moments.

November 25

The large
Tree framing my
Window
Reboots and
Reconnects
My brain and body
With the joy
Only nature
Instills.
The swaying leaves
Create the opportunity
For all tension to
Leave my body
And for this
I am grateful
To the tree in
My window.

Watching the changes in our world from our windows helps connect us to the season and to nature. Each season brings with it special and unique gifts to be thankful for every day.

You may connect with a special tree you watch out a window or flowers on a walk, but make sure you connect to the natural beauty around you. Know that connection to nature provides more than just beauty, also providing a special healing that only nature can provide.

Step outside and observe the miracle of the nature around you. Let nature fill you and connect you with joy. Offer your own prayer of thanks.

November 26

Each being is

Bound to

Experience

Hardship, hurt,

To harbor

Grief,

For grief comes

With living.

Healing of

Body, heart, and spirit

Begins with release

Of hardships

With gratitude

For the hardships

And the gifts

They provide.

As hard as it is to aknowledge, we grow and learn through our hardships. They provide unique moments for us to make needed changes. The process of making these changes is not easy but does provide us with gifts and talents.

Choose to be grateful for the opportunity to learn from your hurt and grief and to develop these gifts and talents. The gratitude will not make you hurt less but does open the opportunity to learn. It also begins the healing process.

Today as you review your hardship and revise your view of this experience, know that you will take gifts and learning from it. Be grateful for the learning. Feel the healing start and know that you will come through the hardship a better human being.

November 27

My body

Is swept with

Waves of tears

Seeping into my

Bones

Until

A feeling

Of rebirth

Centers inside of me

And

I am again

Able to breathe

With gratitude

My body engages

In the world

Again.

We all suffer with loss and grief as a part of life. We also have the choice to allow renewal to emerge from loss. When we do allow renewal, it is joined with deeply felt gratitude for our ability to step forward.

Healing is a choice we make after loss. Being willing to engage in life is scary after a loss and is hard when we are in grief. Part of the healing process starts with knowing you do have things and people to be grateful for each day.

Reflect on a loss that you or someone else has not let go of yet. Determine how you may provide a new way to look at the world with a sense of gratefulness. This will begin the healing process.

November 28

Born with

Joy,

His laughter

Carries through

My heart

Into my life.

I feel his

Kindness

And joy

Shining

In his

Eyes.

My life

Is filled with

Grace and goodness.

A deep and centered gratefulness enters each of us for those who come into our lives with unbridled joy. These people bring joy with their presence, and their joy shines through to our core.

When joyful people cross our paths, it is imperative that we allow them in and learn from them. Joy and gratitude are linked and create a cycle of living that is healthy and positive.

To fill your day with grace and goodness, seek time with joyful people. Be focused and aware of how they behave, and learn to repeat their joy.

November 29

All acts

On behalf of others

Are true

Acts of

Gratitude,

For gratitude

Is future-focused.

Actions of good

For others

Move to your

Own act of

Gratefulness.

Gratitude is engaging in activity for others. Those who have found internal happiness and peace are those who act on their gratitude for others. Of all the activities that connect us, actualized gratitude—giving back—provides the strongest link.

Sharing our own gifts with others increases our ability to be grateful. This active gratitude also builds your capacity for finding grateful moments in your own life.

Today, act on your own gratitude. Do for another without expectation of thanks. Notice how living in gratitude makes you feel, and repeat it. Make a commitment to build your own capacity for gratitude through doing for others.

November 30

No one perfect way

To gain

Enlightenment

Peace

Happiness

But

One powerful

Opener of your

Heart

To the potential

Every time

Is gratitude.

Practicing daily gratitude leads your life down a path of enlightenment about your world, your connections, and yourself. Being grateful for the large and small miracles that cross your path is your guide to internal happiness.

Gratitude opens your heart to the potential in life. The practice of daily gratefulness is a powerful life-changer. It doesn't mean that your struggles go away, but it does mean that you have the potential to frame those struggles differently.

Practice gratitude by finding time in your day to be aware of the good things around you. Daily, say, "Thank you," for the gifts and talents given to you, and today, thank the people who make a difference in the world and to you.

December

As the year comes to a close and a new year advances, it is time to reflect on how we decide to end events, relationships, and periods in our life. We may not control what has happened or everything in our future, but we control how we react to the events and people in our lives.

When we take control of our reactions, we should be aware that we need to embrace the times filled with the unknown. Being able to muddle through a confusing time brings clarity and opens a new beginning with newly discovered options.

While we are ending a year, we are also opening a new one. This month, focus on closing the events of your past with love and with healthy activities. Begin to embrace the muddle of the unknown and to seek clarity to see all your upcoming options and possibilities.

December Focuses

Endings need celebration.

Embrace chaos before beginnings.

Open your heart to possibilities.

December 1

My endings

Have been

Many.

Had thinking

Been reframed

To view the

Ending as a

Possibility,

The ending

Journey

Would have

Been laced

With

Sadness and

Joy.

We all have endings throughout our lives. Some we dread, and some we look forward to. Endings can make us feel sad. Those feelings of sadness are real and need to be recognized, and it is also important that we reframe how we view our endings.

An ending is also a beginning. To fully experience and enjoy new beginnings, we need to formally say good-bye, and we also need to focus our thinking on how we are heading toward new possibility.

Determine what endings you are facing, and allow your feelings to come forward. As you face this new ending, focus on how you will formally and intentionally say good-bye with grace and kindness. As you engage in your good-bye, frame your thinking to begin looking at opportunities for growth and learning. Reach for the possibility.

December 2

The year

Walk-through

Contains

Milestones

Celebrations

Disappointments,

All

Needing closure

And although

Forever marked by

This year,

I seek

My openings,

Wishing to run

Forward

Without a pull from

The past.

As we close out the year, it is time to reflect on our milestones, celebrations, and disappointments. While we sometimes think the focus of closure is on the painful moments of the year, closure is the process of clearing the way for new living and requires us to not live in any of our past, good or bad.

Completing this kind of closure ensures that we are ready to move forward and to not lean on our past accomplishments or harbor past mistakes but to open the door to new options. It can be scary to let go of the past and to move forward to the next adventure without the past holding you back.

Walk through this year and determine what you are holding onto from your past. Closing those events may take several walk-throughs of the year. Closing an event may require writing journal entries or a phoning a friend to talk the event through. Free yourself to be open to new possibilities.

December 3

I enter a
Time
Of ending
But think of the
Next beginning.
Time passed so
Quickly,
I am unable to
Imagine.
In a blink
The world and my life
Rushed by
In pain and pleasure,
But for now,
This moment
Is my most
Precious
For I am
Here.

Our endings stretch into beginnings, but not with a clean break. There is often a time of messy confusion in each ending. We may feel better when we are not in the messy in-between time, but that time offers a gift of thinking and framing both the ending and beginning.

You may find yourself in the in-between time, when you wish to change jobs or determine to move on from a relationship. Any big life change creates an in-between time. Rather than avoid this precious time, be determined to use it to frame how you want to close the door and which door you want to open next.

Everyone has messy periods that are confusing. Try to not avoid the messy time, but use it to bring clarity. Every day, be determined to find your clarity by focusing on what is confusing to you. Be guided by your gut feelings, and explore those feelings by doing some research to determine your next steps.

December 4

A door of one I love

Closed

On me.

The sound

Rings in my

Ears

But I will

Not stay

At the door

Closed

Before me,

Because

It will blind me

To the doors

Being opened

And block the

Gentle breeze

Touching

My ears.

It is difficult to close a relationship, whether it is closed by choice or by circumstance. We desire to hold on to those who have left us, and it is difficult to leave the doors that have closed. We should not linger at closed doors because they blind us from the other opportunities placed along our journey.

Realize that even with the door closed, the person has not left us. Our experiences and memories of the person can be honored and help us with our new experiences. The person is always part of you but should never hold you stagnant.

Today, think about those people who have moved forward and closed doors on their time with you. Determine if you are still standing at their doors or are aware of the opportunities being opened for you. Honor your past relationships for the learning provided, and walk through your new door.

December 5

Slow and tiny

Buds pop

Above the dirt,

Benefitting

From

Prior

Growth,

Which had its

Own time

And now provides

The foundation

To a new beginning

Needed in a new

Way.

The new bud

Wobbles

With support.

As you end one chapter, make sure that your leaving allows those who follow you to have a good foundation. Ending is not about pulling up your roots and leaving but about providing a foundation to support those needing to fill your spot.

When we are ready to leave to start new opportunities, we often want to leave quietly with no fanfare. Although fanfare may not be necessary, preparing others to sustain your work is necessary. The continuation of your work will change, but your foundation will sustain the continuation.

Begin today to ensure that those following you will have the skills and abilities to not only continue but also improve your work. Even if your leaving is far off, be proactive with building your support people whom your leaving will create a beginning.

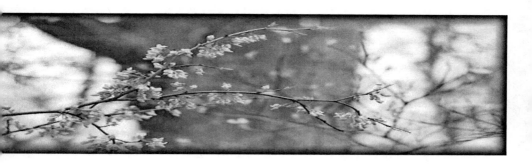

December 6

Events of life
Flow into
Each other,
Making
It difficult
To manage
The shift
From an
Ending to
A new start.
At times,
The swift
Flow moves
Without us being
Aware,
But know that
Endings
Whirlpool
Back, returning us
Until
We say
Good-bye.

It might be easier if life's events were marked as beginnings and endings, but life's events flow and shift sometimes make it difficult to have neat and tidy endings and clean openings, and we have to muddle through the messiness of life.

While navigating the flow of life, we often miss an ending or get so caught up in opening a new part of life that the ending passes without the closure we need. But some endings need a formal closing and resurface throughout our lives until we find closure.

Think about the issues that you are dealing with that keep resurfacing. Reflect on what keeps popping up for you, and deal with it in a healthy way. Determine how you might face the issue, and give it closure.

December 7

Determined to
Fully heal,
I know
I must crawl
Under the rug,
Wrapped to
Feel
And fill my
Soul,
Then like a
Butterfly
Feel the
Freedom and
Emerge,
Able to feel
Joy.

To fully heal, we must turn over the rug under which we have swept those things we find hard to face. Healing is an ongoing process and begins with us dealing with our troubles in a healthy way. When we do this, we can emerge able to feel joy.

It can be scary to face those hurts that affect our ability to feel full joy. Sometimes we need help with our journey of healing, and sometimes when we really look at the issue holding us back, we find it is no longer so bad. Either way, we all need to face issues that hurt us.

You are worthy of feeling joy. Begin to examine the hurts that hold you back. If you need help, seek it out today. If you can work through the pain, start that journey today by allowing the feelings to surface.

December 8

Nourish the beginning.
It is in need
Of protection.
It will develop,
Beginning sprouts
Through being
Filled with
The spirit of
Life's goodness.
Allow your beginning
To grow
And create new
Seeds
For continuation.

Whatever your beginning is—whether a new friendship, a new job, or a new idea—it must be protected and care for with intention. We often take for granted that our new starts will be fine with time, but our new starts are better with care.

The way we nourish beginnings can be different with each new start, but make time for nourishing to make a solid foundation. Time is one of our most precious resources, so making time for your new beginning is a great start. Be attentive, listening and responding to your new adventure.

Today, be intentional in giving time to your new beginning. Remember, you are providing a foundation for the new seeds you have just planted, and they need care.

December 9

Endings are not

Bad

But are the signal of

New

Beginnings.

Endings, middles, beginnings

Are melded

Into our journeys.

We navigate

Through

Life,

Learning

To navigate

Each and

To create a richer

Experience.

We often dread endings, but an ending is simply a signal of a new opportunity beginning. Our journeys can be richer if we approach our endings as new beginnings.

Navigating daily life is a learning process. Being open to the endings as well as to the time before beginnings, when there is confusion, is necessary to a productive new start. The messy and unclear times that occur before you are sure of your direction offer the gift of learning.

Today, think about how open you are to your journey of endings, middles, and beginnings. Being open means you can embrace the pain and opportunities that a journey brings. Be determined to open yourself to each stage you find yourself experiencing.

December 10

In slow, deep
Breathing
I find
A neutral
Place
Of learning.
Without the
Breathing
In place,
It seems
Messy and
Unorganized,
But stopping to
Breathe
Allows to me
To take advantage
Of messy thinking
Prior to starting
A new beginning.

The messy, chaotic parts of life can make us feel buried, but these times also make us think about what we want, and we need to recognize them as valuable learning time.

We often try to hurry through such a period rather than embracing the learning opportunity it provides. When we hurry through this messy period, we may move to a beginning that is not on the path we would have taken if we had used the chaotic time to find clarity.

Take a deep breath and get ready to embrace the times in your life when you are unsure of your next steps. Be aware that such times of uncertainty are gifts. Seek clarity and embrace your time of learning.

December 11

Closing the circle,

Shutting the door,

Finishing the chapter.

It matters not what

We call our ending.

It does matter

That we recognize

And honor

Moments in life

That have reached a stop,

For we no longer

Can live in those

Moments

But can take forward

Our learning

While letting

The past

Fly free

In the wind.

When a part of life comes to a close, we may feel sad at the loss, and this feeling can overwhelm us. Although sad feelings are normal, we need to take time to honor the path that has come to a close.

Even our painful journeys need to be honored, because they provide learning and make us better people. Honoring and closing those life moments allow us to move forward with learning rather than with pain.

Think about how you are honoring your closures and turning them from sad events to learning events. Honor all events in your life, and make sure they make you better.

December 12

I honor the
Journey I
Take daily
By taking time
To celebrate
The events
And people
Crossing my
Journey path
And leaving their
Imprint
Of living.
Time together
Was short
And paths
Diverged.
I celebrate the
Time and
The ending.

Some people enter your life and then fade out after a time. Although we can miss those people, we should know that they left us better people. We can also honor the imprint they left when they passed through our lives.

Celebrating, honoring, and allowing closure to the people and events of your past creates a good place to move forward to without sadness. Although the time you had together has ended, taking time to wish those people happiness is helpful to you in letting them go. It also allows you a new perspective of those moving through your life now.

Reflect on those friends or colleagues who have crossed your path and have moved on to new adventures. If you miss them but know there is no reconnecting, wish them well and celebrate what you shared. Let them go with love.

December 13

Transitioning

A mindset, an emotion, a habit

Messy, uncomfortable, jarring,

Which no change

Happens without

A transition demands

Moving toward

And embracing

An unknown

Period of white fuzziness

Soft edges and instability

Let it be

Examination of new possibility at the new year is normal; however, we often determine that the transition will be painful and that we are not ready, or we are afraid.

Take on one transition at a time and understand the messy process you are entering. Full living with yourself and those you love is a process requiring engagement with messy feelings. Full engagement means not knowing, and it may feel as if you are not on solid ground.

In a stage of transition, we are unsure and nothing is clear. We have to muddle through this period to make sense of the change. If you are afraid of the unknown and wish everything to be clear all the time, you will be unable to change. Settle into the fuzzy, and let the world clear for your thinking to come into focus.

December 14

Life transitioning

Is a skill

To be practiced

Throughout our lives,

As we should

Never

Stop making

Changes

In who

We are

And how

We practice

Life.

We teach many skills to our children in order for them to navigate through life. One skill often over looked is being able to transition with healthy grace. We can teach it by modeling the graceful transition through life's closures.

Transitioning with healthy grace requires us to allow a time of unknown and, in the stillness, to allow clarity to emerge. It means we have to be open to not knowing the answer but believing that options will become clear and choices will be presented.

We need to model the skill of being open to the unknown and the willingness to find moments of still thinking for those we love. Today, explain your openness to moving into unknown territory to someone you think could benefit from the conversation. Take time with that person to be still in thinking and to believe the options will be forthcoming.

December 15

My anticipation
Of opening doors
Overflows with
With gratitude
For the door
Being placed
In my journey.
While there is
Unknown,
I realize
My past
Journey
Has prepared me
For the difficult
Opportunities
That I
Will open with
Joy.

We need to pause to be thankful for the many opportunities that are open to us. Although it is true we might not fully know what is facing us with each choice, we are blessed to have the opportunity in front of us.

When we are centered and balanced in life, we are ready to see the possibilities that are open to us. Our past prepares us for what is in store during our next adventures.

Today, be grateful for your own past opportunities and have confidence that you are ready to open your new opportunities. Give thanks for your learning, for it has prepared you for your next adventure.

December 16

I determine
My own
Story
With my
Choices
In how
I greet
Each beginning
And approach
My farewells.
While I control
Only a part of my
Story,
I will write it
With honor
And play it
To my best.

Although beginnings and endings are part of our ongoing work, we have the power to write our own stories, including the endings and beginnings. There is power in taking ownership of your choices with each beginning and farewell.

Writing your story requires a willingness to be aware of the whole story and to gain inclusive perspectives with a focus on truth. When we look at the whole story and listen to other perspectives, we can write our stories with our hearts and become better at greeting beginnings and approaching good-byes.

Today, think about your story. Who is writing it? Does it include the whole story and other perspectives? Does it focus on the truth? Determine how writing your own story can help you with your beginnings and endings.

December 17

Find order in chaos.

Uncover confusion in

What seems to

Be order.

Chaos is a

Place

We find

Ourselves in

When trying

To close and open

Parts of our lives.

Although chaos

May feel scratchy,

It serves the

Purpose

Of cleansing us

To live with

Intention.

The times in life that are uncertain provide an opportunity for clarity when we are closing one part of life and opening a new one. Engaging in the uncertain moments of life can be a struggle but is worth the learning that comes with struggling to find clarity.

We often try to avoid struggling, but struggling makes us better. Going forward into what seems chaos allows us to find real order in our lives. This starts us toward living life with intention and purpose.

Be determined to engage with the chaos order to sort your way to thinking clearly about where you want to start again. You may need help to work through the uncertain times, so be willing to reach out to someone who can help. What may feel scratchy serves a purpose.

December 18

Waves remind me

With repeating

Crashing

Of the ongoing

Process that

Life engages

Me in.

With the

Constant

Change of

Each wave,

I am still

Able to see

The ocean

Horizon

And know

The possibility

Waiting for

Me.

Life is filled with constant change, and we can be buried by the onslaught of each crashing change. It is important while coping with change that we look up long enough to see the possibilities on the horizon in front of us.

Change comes at us daily, with some changes being life-altering and some just tweaks in the day. Transitioning through changes requires us to be flexible, resilient, and positive. Change is constant, and our skills of transition need to be sharp if we are to meet possibility.

With all of the changes that rush toward you, become aware of your own skills of flexibility, resiliency, and positive attitude. Which of these skills do you need to improve? Select one to work on during the coming year. Check on your progress monthly by thinking of how your actions have been flexible, resilient, and positive.

December 19

Although the world

Brings me

Surprises

I still choose

How I engage in

Endings

Put before me

And

How I greet

New beginnings,

Providing

A slice

Of control

Where

Life happens

Living a full life continually brings changes, and some of them are complete surprises. Although you often have no control over the surprises life has brought your way, you still control how you engage in the ending and how you greet a new beginning.

I can be thoughtful and look at the impact of the change on myself and others. Taking time to breathe and to accept what is in front of me, I can be aware of others and their reactions. I can look for the positive in what is coming, and I can focus on new possibility. These are my choices.

Reflect on how you choose to engage in your own life's surprises. What are you choosing to focus on? Spend time adjusting how you chose to react to surprises or changes in your life. Write down how you want to react, and keep it near so you can be reminded.

December 20

The door stands
My time is now
I wish to walk through quickly
With no good-bye.
I touch what can never be touched
Again,
Each moment savored for the
Comfortable.
I brace inside the door for the last
Moment,
And then with intention
I walk through to the
Unknown.

Transitioning is difficult and requires a process or an ending ceremony. When we complete a transition without a proper good-bye, we often find ourselves standing in the same doorway again and again.

As you transition, allow yourself to use all your senses to say good-bye and to savor what was good while knowing that standing in a doorway, in between, does not all allow for full living.

Although we often do not know what is beyond the doorjamb, completing a good-bye ceremony allows us a healthy step into the unknown. We are often afraid of the intense emotions of good-byes, but allow these emotions with touches, smiles, and tears. Walk through the doorway with intention.

December 21

The spirit of

Hope

Circles me

And holds my hand.

With a deep

Breath, I

Push forward

Through

Sad thinking.

I feel her

Strengthening

My resolve

To step into

A future

Of new beginnings

And I know that

With

Hope,

I am not

Alone.

With hope, we can end and begin new chapters in life with a positive focus. We need to cultivate hopefulness in life by being aware of our thinking and redirecting it when it moves to negativity. Hope helps us move forward to possibility.

Allowing hope to be part of your daily thinking will help you feel that you are not alone. Feeling hopeful in the hard times is difficult but necessary. Hope is not a feeling that just comes to you; it is a process you work toward every day.

Be determined today to work toward being hopeful in your present moment and for your future opportunities. Take a moment today to picture what you would be doing if you were hopeful. Move toward that picture with actions.

December 22

The hardest part
Of being
My change
In the world
Is believing
My small
Part of
Creating
Change in
The world matters—
Until
I remember that
A new way
Of living
Starts with
One person
Opening
A door
For others
To peek
At possibility.

Changing yourself is difficult, and changing the world may seem impossible, but the world changes by people changing themselves. It starts with one person believing and then doing.

Mahatma Gandhi told us to be the change we want to see in the world. That change starts with us doing and believing that we can change ourselves and the world. When we do, we open doors of possibility for others.

Start your day today thinking about the change you want to see in the world. What will you need to change in yourself to make the change in the world? Tell one other person your plan.

December 23

The time before

A new

Beginning

Leaps with

Imagination

And dreams

Of what

Is possible.

It is in this

Time we create

The plans

And lay foundations

To build

The next layer

Of life.

Be an architect,

Not a bricklayer.

We are often in a rush to get the next thing started, but before starting a new phase, we often are in our most creative thinking. Being able to dream of possibility and to use your imagination for creating plans for the future is a gift.

This is valuable time if we tap into it and nurture it. We have the ability to lay the foundation and to design our next ideas. We don't need to always lay the bricks for someone else's plan.

Give yourself time to dream, and be ambitious with your thinking. What is out there that you want to do? Begin to lay the foundation for your dreams. Dreams are made by thinkers who do. Begin.

December 24

Possibilities
Opportunities
Curiosity—
Words to
Invest in
And believe,
For the curious
See doors of
Opportunity
And open
Doors,
Creating the
Possibility
For new
Paths.

It is rejuvenating to invest in possibility, opportunity, and curiosity. If we believe in these ideas and act to make these words become part of our reality, we open positive doors to our future.

Much is possible when we put our minds to believing in ourselves and that we have many options available to us. Once we believe, we need to act on our possibilities. They can become reality.

Today, work at investing in yourself by examining your ability to see possibilities and opportunities, and by engaging in curiosity. If you are unable to see and engage, ask a person close to you to help you see your possibilities and opportunities. Then be curious enough to investigate what work would be required for you to realize your options.

December 25

I draw on
Strength from
A baby's story
That had a
Beginning and
An end
Filled with choices
Of faith,
Believing
That both the ending
And the beginning
Filled the world
With
Possibility.
It is my hope
To walk in
These steps with
My own beginnings
And ending to
Also fill the
World with
Possibility.

Each of us has a beginning and an end, but it is the journey that can make an impact on the world and the people we love. Our choices create positive possibility for those following us to grow and learn.

Great opportunity exists for you to walk your own journey toward helping others. Whatever your journey has been, today, you can walk a new path, because we can begin each day anew and end each day with the promise of a new beginning.

Today, whatever your faith, take a moment to gain strength from a baby's story and know that you have a journey to walk. You can fill the world with possibility one step at a time.

December 26

His door closed
So long ago,
But my journey
Though his
Path
Opened
A hundred new
Paths
And helped
In creating
Who I
Am today.
I honor
That path
And press my hand
On his closed door,
Hoping
He honors
The path too.

Some people are part of who you are and made your life better and made you a better person because you learned from them, and for whatever reason, they moved out of your life. We can celebrate those relationships that have taught us how to be in relationship.

Even those relationships that ended badly have purpose in your life, and you can learn from them. Without bitterness, you can ensure learning. As you learn from closed relationships, you can be a healthy partner.

For those people whom you have left in your past, find a moment of quiet reflection in which to put your hand on their closed doors and give thanks for what they brought to your life to make you a stronger, happier person.

December 27

The words
Read to
Affirm
Have meaning
Only when you act on
The possibility.
If the words
Inspire you
To walk through
A new door,
You have affirmed
Your
Life.

Saying or writing the right words is only the beginning of living with full energy and balance. Giving the words meaning through your actions is what is important. To affirm your life, you need to think, say, and do the words given to you.

It is good to invest time in meditation and affirmation, but living with actions aligned to those silent moments moves us forward in life. Let the words used in meditation inspire you to action.

Take action on one of the affirmations that has touched your heart. Do it today. Your action can be small or large, but begin your new thinking with working toward it.

December 28

Barriers,

Obstacles, and problems

Are personal teachers

Giving opportunity to

Possibility

And providing

Gateways to wisdom

And learning,

Which I am

Willing to

Walk through

In order to open

My life

To a

New beginning

With new wisdom

And learning.

Our teachers sometimes come in the form of our problems. Those obstacles, though painful, allow us to learn and gain life's wisdom. Those problems that teach you important lessons can help you begin a new chapter as a better person.

We often avoid our problems or try to get through them quickly. We need to become reflective during and after our problems. Allowing learning to occur requires being open to the lessons in our problems.

Think about your latest obstacle or problem. Reflect on what you learned from the experience. Open your mind and heart beyond the hurt to the learning, and be determined to reflect during and after your next problem.

December 29

The vast possibility

Of the future

Becomes our

Reality and

Our responsibility

Once we

Open the door.

Walk through

With courage

And grace.

Reality and

Responsibility

Merge and

Create

Our lives.

Your possibilities are waiting for you to open the door and commit to walking through with courage. Our dreams and hopes can become reality when we decide to go forward with the responsibility to work to make them happen.

It is important to remember that possibilities are waiting for you. You can engage in a possibility, but not without work, commitment, and persistence. You need to be determined to open the door and walk through toward your options.

Make it possible for your dreams to become your reality. Take ownership of working to make your dreams come true. Post the steps you need to do to make things come to reality in a place you see them daily. Talk to someone about your steps to clarify your thinking.

December 30

Hopeful people are

Uncertain about

Their futures

But open to

All coming

Paths and possibilities.

There is full-on

Dedication

To change

From the

Bottoms of

Of their

Hearts

To the tips of

Their fingers,

Working in unison

To realize

Hope.

People who maintain hope do not know more than anyone else; they just remain open to what the future holds for them and believe that they will be able to deal with what comes their way. They are dedicated to transitioning into the new options.

It is important to have belief and hope in your heart as well as to be active in transitioning your surroundings and yourself. Both believing and acting will move you forward with positivity.

Be reflective and thoughtful about your life transitions. Are you hopeful about your coming options? How are you using your heart and hands to help in your transition? Make adjustments in your level of hope in order to assist in your next transition.

December 31

Closing this year,
I recognize
The growth
In my heart
And in my
My wisdom bank,
But I open
My new year
Knowing
My best work
Is yet
To be
And the world
Is opening
Arms
To my next
Possibility.
Determined,
I embrace
The coming
Options.

Closing out a year requires acknowledgment of the growth and learning we have experienced in it. There is a great deal to be proud of from the year. This is also the time to realize that your best work is yet to come.

When you know the world is open to you, you have more to learn, and this enables you to create new goals that challenge and stretch you. Just knowing there is more waiting for you to discover is important to starting a new year.

Close out this year with a reflection on what you have learned in your heart and head. Take a moment to give thanks for all learning, and then move your thoughts to your options and possibilities for the coming year. Know that your best work is yet is be.

Dr. Webb lives in Arizona but also spends time at her house on the Oregon coast. She and her husband enjoy their family but especially their grandchildren, who are also learning be aware of the world around them and how they can make their part of the world better. Her practice in mindfulness is a daily process requiring intention and restarts to be centered and balanced in her work and play. Through her practice she finds daily joy.

CPSIA information can be obtained
at www.ICGtesting.com
Printed in the USA
FSOW02n0213270517
34537FS